TIME

FROM FAMINE TO FEAST

Reading *Time: From Famine to Feast* felt like sitting down over a cup of tea to work through some of my deepest concerns about how to live a meaningful life with one of the wisest women I know. Packed full of poignant observations about how we can befriend, tend and spend our most precious resource, Donna Schaper leads us on a spiritual quest for "personal coherence" with wit, humor and some serious "aha" moments. This insightful, practical and efficient book is a must-read for anyone seeking new ways to dig out of your deadening time hole and "calmly plot your resurrection." – Jennifer Crumpton, Author of *Femmevangelical: The Modern Girl's Guide to the Good News*

Time: From Famine to Feast will change your view of time, and quite possibly the quality of your life. This is one of the best books for congregational teaching that I have ever read. It has the power to change lives. The title says it is about time. It is really about life and meaning. You will experience more of both if you heed its wisdom. – Rev. Alexander E. Sharp, Executive Director, Clergy for a New Drug Policy

Donna Schaper writes about life in a way that challenges, excites and ultimately inspires. – Douglas Beane, Playwright

Time: From Famine to Feast came just in the knick of time! There is not a conversation that goes by where I don't find myself talking with someone about how busy, stressed, overwhelmed, inundated, and frenzied they feel. Technology has resulted in a new unspoken rule that says we are to be constantly available and never turn off. But the world is ready for some new rules – rules that protect our spirit, our fun, and our health. I love Donna Schaper's totally practical and spiritually based view. And I love her challenge to all of us to shift our perspective and to make different choices. Challenge accepted! I am already crafting my new time feast! – Carissa Reiniger, Founder/CEO, Silver Lining

The clock shown on the front and back covers and overleaf is at the Musée d'Orsay in Paris, France.

DONNA SCHAPER

TIME
From Famine to Feast

WOOD LAKE

Editor: Mike Schwartzentruber
Designer: Robert MacDonald
Proofreader: Dianne Greenslade

Library and Archives Canada Cataloguing in Publication
Schaper, Donna, author
Time : from famine to feast / Donna Schaper.
Issued in print and electronic formats.
ISBN 978-1-77064-811-1 (paperback).- ISBN 978-1-77064-812-8 (html)
1. Time management - Religious aspects - Christianity. I. Title.
BV4598.5.S33 2016   248.4   C2015-907341-3   C2015-907342-1

Copyright © 2016 Wood Lake Publishing Inc.
All rights reserved. No part of this publication may be reproduced – except in the case of brief quotations embodied in critical articles and reviews – stored in an electronic retrieval system, or transmitted in any form or by any means, electronic, mechanical, photocopying, recording, or otherwise, without prior written permission of the publisher or copyright holder.

ISBN 978-1-77064-811-1

Published by Wood Lake Publishing Inc.
485 Beaver Lake Road, Kelowna, BC, Canada, V4V 1S5
www.woodlake.com | 250.766.2778

We acknowledge the financial support of the Government of Canada. Nous reconnaissons l'appui financier du gouvernement du Canada. Wood Lake Publishing acknowledges the financial support of the Province of British Columbia through the Book Publishing Tax Credit.

At Wood Lake Publishing, we practice what we publish, being guided by a concern for fairness, justice, and equal opportunity in all of our relationships with employees and customers. Wood Lake Publishing is committed to caring for the environment and all creation. Wood Lake Publishing recycles and reuses, and encourages readers to do the same. Books are printed on 100% post-consumer recycled paper, whenever possible. A percentage of all profit is donated to charitable organizations.

Printed in Canada
Printing 10 9 8 7 6 5 4 3 2 1

TABLE OF CONTENTS

INTRODUCTION
Never Enough Time / 7

CHAPTER ONE
The Tangle that Keeps Us in the Time Famine / 11

CHAPTER TWO
"Real" Technology and Spiritual Technology / 23

CHAPTER THREE
The Work-Family Dilemma / 35

CHAPTER FOUR
A Recipe for Feast: Writing Your Personal Coherence / 47

CHAPTER FIVE
When Feast Becomes Fun / 59

CHAPTER SIX
Down-and-Dirty How To: From Famine to Feast in 52 Weeks / 71

CONCLUSION
Guidelines for Small Groups / 83

INTRODUCTION

Never Enough Time

Say the words "time famine" and people immediately know what you mean. Some people call the time famine "time poverty," or the "time suck." Others call it the war against rest. Still others just whine, "I don't have enough time. I never have enough time." We could imagine these complaints as fear of mortality. Of course we don't have enough time. We get the days we get. But more pervasively, these complaints are practical statements. I have more to do than I have *time* in which to do it. I want *more* than I can get in the time I am allotted. That is the time famine. It involves our consent to a scarcity metaphor for life, one that we set up ourselves by not defining what we mean by *more*, *less*, and *enough*.

The time famine becomes a deeper disease as well. It goes viral. It turns a spiritual and psychological corner after it attacks our calendars, sleeping habits, and even our lunch practices. *The New York Times* recently published an article showing how people no longer do business lunches. A quick portable coffee will do.

And it's not just this week or next week during which we don't have enough time. The time famine is the despair that develops around our singed edges. It is the feeling that we may *never* have enough time. We may *never* get through what we need to do. We may *always* feel this way. Such experiences make us sad. The experience of the time famine erodes our desire and stamina for self-improvement. We find that we no longer bother with New

Year's resolutions. We imagine that we are stuck in famine. This "stuckness" hurts and saps our spirits, and it goes on to sap the spirit of our cultures and our families, our children and our parents. Evidence mounts that the time famine is no longer just for people who have three part-time jobs. The time famine is an equal-opportunity employer, engaging the upper, middle, and working classes, as well as all age groups.

Time feast

Systemic change rarely comes from stuck and sapped people, and this very lack of systemic change gives the time famine a curious permission to persist. So this book is not just about the time famine. The opposite of a time famine is a "time feast." It is like feeling rich rather than poor, unencumbered rather than encumbered. Instead of feeling poor, residing in a country called scarcity, we feel rich and reside in a country called wealth. We become like octogenarian Warren Buffet, the billionaire who swears he tap dances to work every day.

This book is also about the importance of *aim*. Very few of us *aim* to have the time famine; most of us just endure it. We also know that if we don't prioritize our life, someone else will happily do it for us. We are taught "you can have it all," even though we know this is a despairing form of nonsense. Here I want to take the winding, interacting tendrils off our bodies and lives and *aim* for *feast*. I want to show both how the time famine is "done" to us, and how we do it to ourselves. I want to move beyond the posture of victim into the posture of victor.

I am not saying we can cure ourselves of the time famine. That would be hubris. The powers that be really are the powers that be. The systems that hurt us really like our despairing passivity. Instead, I offer a spiritual solution to the time famine. I am *aiming* for spiritual non-participation. We *do* have control over our spirits, if not the systems that surround them.

I don't personally know anybody who doesn't live some version of the time famine. Even people with too much time on their hands, the unemployed or those very late in life, say they wish they could fill time with something good for themselves or for others. It is difficult to find a retiree who thinks they have enough time in their day. But here's the thing. When we realize that we are in good company, sometimes we find a bit of comradeship, if not liberation. Recognizing the extent of the time famine helps us aim our way out of it.

Aiming for feast is the point. It is very nice to know where you are going and then to arrive there. You might even call the takeoff and landing at the intended place *happiness*. Or *focus*. In the good life, we take off at fuzzy and land at focused. We don't put up with famine, especially because we don't have to. *We arrive at feast by aiming for it*. Like a good pitcher, we aim for home plate. A less able pitcher throws the ball and hits first base. Or third base. A good writer hits a target. A less able writer starts off fuzzy and lands at fuzzy.

Some of us self-hijack. We agree to the terms of the famine rather than aim to change them. Instead of taking off and landing at the destination we intend, we participate in going off track and ending up where we don't want to be. We participate in how bad we feel by consenting to it.

Here I try to break the systemic and personal cycle of the time famine. In previous books, I have said that keeping a Sabbath is a form of civil disobedience. In this book, I add spiritual practices to Sabbath-keeping. I aim for feast – practically, spiritually, on the job, at home, and in our hopes for a coherent life; a life in which we are the driver and not the driven.

CHAPTER ONE

The Tangle that Keeps Us in the Time Famine

The systemic sources that keep us tangled in the time famine have been well documented by dozens of sociologists. Juliet Schor started with *The Overworked American*. She documented the unexpected decline of leisure. Benjamin Kline Hunnicut followed with *Work without End*. *The Economist* magazine has discussed "time poverty" and *Time* magazine asked the plaintive question, "Why is everybody so busy?" *Time* answered its own question saying that we are genuinely more busy *and* that we *perceive* that we are more busy.

I want to reverse *Time*'s astute analysis and say that we can also perceive our way to a greater sense of *enough*. If perception is one root of the time famine and if we *do* control some of our perception, why can't perception or reimagining ourselves as drivers rather than as driven not also provide a way out?

The question of fault and blame – and their accomplice shame – arises immediately. Is it my fault that I don't have enough time? Is it the system's fault or capitalism's fault?

Some blame the political economy that doles out prizes for hard work and blames the genuinely poor for their poverty. "If only they would work harder," we say, "then they wouldn't be poor." The cousin to this argument is applied to everyone, sneakily, and not just to the poor. "If only we would work harder, then we wouldn't be so time starved."

The relationship between effort and virtue has been with us since the Industrial Revolution spawned the Protestant Reformation and its work ethic. Or the Protestant Reformation spawned the Industrial Revolution. Either way you see it, effort became a virtue and laziness a sin. Now, as we enter a new global revolution, with a new accompanying theology and spirituality, we discover that being "connected" is taking the place of effort. This translates to being "bad" if you don't keep up with emails, or if you become separated from your cell phone, a modern rosary if there ever was one.

The causes of the time famine are large. They are systemic. They have to do with the way we work and how most of us commute to work. They have to do with the way we raise our children and never feel that we are giving them "enough." They have to do with the way *more* and *better* took over our hearts as leading values. More and better replaced *enough* as drivers of our thinking and being.

But I don't want to talk about the *causes* of the time famine in political, economic, or social terms. I want to talk about them in terms of the *inner way*, the way we have internalized the commandments of multiple systems and feel bad or wrong or in violation or out of compliance if we don't obey our orders to be busy, active, connected, overworked, and time famished.

You could call my approach a spiritual solution to a large material problem. Or you could call it a spirituality of holy leisure. Or a "Sabbath-plus" way of life. Or a resacralization of the way time has become desacralized. Or a way to turn work into play.

Spirit is larger than systems

The initial antidote to famine is first food and water, stingily dispensed. But the *real* antidote is feast, and that is ours whenever we want it, as creatures of a God who graced us with life.

When we say we "don't have enough time," we are actually saying something deeply spiritual. Yes, we are going to die. That reality, as much as we try to bury it with clutter and texting, lies beneath the time famine. We are going to die. We won't have enough time. Our only hope against that terrible if awesome mystery is to live the time feast now. When we *don't* live in our own time, our few days on this earth, we die prematurely. We refuse the grace of God that brought us here in the first place. But if we live the time feast now, death can't possibly hurt us. Spiritual freedom comes from facing death *and living*.

Spiritual freedom also requires a long hard look at why we obey our masters – those of the clock, the hourly "wage," and the homogenization of time. Part of my spiritual solution or method for moving from the land of time famine to the land of time feast involves repenting the "sin" of internalizing capitalism. The time famine is not the sin. The sin is our participation in it.

By sin I mean missing the mark of our humanity, being distant from the Divine, or being *Incurvatus in se*, Martin Luther's wonderful definition of sin as being curved in on oneself. All of these forms or expressions of sin have to die, along with the perception that we are more important than we are and that God is less important than God is.

When we consent to the time famine, we forget or ignore that we are human *beings*, not human *doings*. When we consent to the time famine, we become distant from that splash of surprise, or jingle of joy, or glimpse of grace that reminds us that God is nigh. We forget to praise, or we wander around town with our yoga mat slung over our arm and a grimace on our face. We act like God did not create us, or that God does not reside in our next breath. My friend tells me she loves her yoga class but can't stand the breathing part. She just wants them to "get on with it." Such impatience, when the possibility of praise surrounds! When we consent to the time famine, we get curved in on ourselves. We forget to look up, or at the person sitting across from us in the restaurant. That old *New Yorker* cartoon comes to mind. Instead of asking "Smoking or not smoking?" as the couple walks in, the waiter asks, "Phoning or not phoning?"

Like I said, the time famine is not the sin. The sin is our participation in it. The sin is our *perception* of it – and our *perception* of ourselves.

Our power to choose

The scariest thing I ever touched was not a spider or a snake or my family's frog or a jellyfish in the sea. The scariest thing I ever touched was my power to choose wellness or illness, happiness or sorrow, chocolate or black raspberry, to sleep longer or to wake sooner, to use a carrot or a stick, to stand my ground or to be flexible, to live for myself or for others, to tell my son he is selfish or my husband that he is missing my boat. Usually I choose some version of both and become powerless in the process. When we refuse to choose, we end up in the double-dutch game of trying to live the life *we* want, while also trying to live the life *they* want. Double dutch is when you skip two jump ropes at once. It is tiring to do that, especially when one rope is so much fun to jump all by itself. "Choosing both" is lethal. It puts us out of the driver's seat in our own life. Somebody or something else steers us. We find that we are *driven* in the true sense of that word. Again, I call that sin, missing the mark. We get stained by sin. The ink stains your fingers, as one choice after another that we make, or refuse to make, makes us who we are. The ink of centuries stains our fingers. Does the ink come out? That is the kind of question the time famine uses to plague us. Will things ever be different? Will we ever have a day when we are the person we want to be, when we receive the gift of creation to be who we are?

My friend said she had a good birthday and I asked what made it good. "Because I was the person I want to be all day long." Good answer, right?

Another friend has rapidly advancing MS. When I asked her recently how it was going, she said, "I am living the life I choose."

I pushed. "So much choice has been taken away from you."

She pushed back. "I am living the life I choose in the circumstances I have."

Another good answer. Each person answered back feast to famine.

The "How" of It

Here's a summary of the method I suggest. It is spiritual in the first beat and practical in the second. The practical observances of non-participation become spiritual wealth, breaking the cycle of entrapment to time and opening us to another way.

Shift your time "frame"

Consider daylight saving time. Daylight saving time went into effect in the United States for the first time in 1918, but Benjamin Franklin was the first person to come up with the idea of changing our clocks to take advantage of the longer days. He was serving as a delegate in Paris in 1784 and noticed that Parisians tended to sleep late in the mornings. He wrote a tongue-in-cheek essay arguing that sunlight was going to waste in the mornings and would be much more appreciated in the evenings. By changing the clocks and shifting the daylight hours later, he wrote, people could take advantage of more natural light and save money on candles and lamp oil.

Likewise, some of the spiritual "trick" in time feasting involves changing your clock and changing the way you see your clock. Caroline Woolard, an artist, is building a clock at our church. This clock, called "The 99-Year Movement," has a 99-year dial that counts in 1-year increments, making one full revolution every 99 years. By counting days and years rather than seconds and minutes, Woolard says that this timepiece "aims to honour the movements in land trusts." She is trying to help us think environmentally, artistically, and immortally. She wants the long view and so do most of us. When we have a longer view – or even a playful attitude about time – we are already living in the feast.

In other words, a lot depends on how we *frame* or *perceive* our experience of time. The first step, then, in moving from time famine to time feast is to refuse to believe that the time famine is inevitable. Every chance you get, question the system that put you into speed-up mode in the first place. Withdraw permission from those who say, "this is the way it is," or "this is the best possible world." Do so gently. Keep a smile on your face when you question those who abuse power. Do not combat or fight the time famine! Go Judo on it. Transform its energy into *your* energy. Throw back positive energy on its negative energy. Perceive what you had been perceiving and then re-perceive it. Make a habit of re-perceiving.

Keep a Sabbath

Originally, Jews kept Sabbath for a full day in order to keep their culture together during the Diaspora, when they lost their land and homes and had to wander. For centuries, many Jews and Christians set aside a day of the week for rest in imitation of God's seventh day in the creation story. Six days we work, on the seventh we rest. Today, we no longer work agriculturally, nor even industrially. More and more, we work online. Those of us privileged enough to work the "old way," in the field or from 9 to 5 weekdays, can probably still keep a weekly Sabbath. Many of us cannot, however, and find ourselves ready for a spiritual transition for the new work realities we face.

Also, since the invention of the electric light bulb, we have been able to be awake more and more. We adjust light and clocks and no longer imitate nature's rhythms of night and day. Our sleep is changed and we are unlikely to "day dream," or to have visions in our half sleep, or simply to lie down staring at the stars in the sky. We have evolved to manipulate our sleep with "alarm" clocks, a notion that would make the ancients laugh. We are out of compliance with the natural order by the way we work.

Action and reflection, grace and works, doing and being: humans need rest and peace as much as we need agency and affiliation. We were built that way. Rest is in our DNA. Honouring our need for Sabbath rest is a way of keeping the seventh day in a world that homogenizes time.

So refuse to be naive about the importance of Sabbath-keeping. Keeping a little Sabbath – whether it is Sunday or Saturday worship, an evening truly "off," or a ten-minute daily meditation that empties your brain – is a form of civil disobedience, and spiritual civil disobedience is another step on the way out of the time famine into time feast.

What is a little Sabbath? It is a time when you are down, not up; receiving, not giving; being, not doing. It is time set apart that is different from ordinary time. It is departure from your allotted time into God's time, which is as much your home as your allotted time is. It is special time, when we reflect on our actions and let them seep into our souls. Sabbath is moving into the eternal from the daily, to a little bit of heaven from a lot of earth. It is sacred time. Sacred time is the time of praise and gratitude. It is not measured in minutes and hours but in something larger, as big as eternity. Ashes to ashes, stardust to stardust, I like to say.

Befriend your mortality ... and *live*

Many of us act as though time is this big fat fixed thing that oppresses us. We perceive time as untouchable, unmanageable, as having its own immortality while we don't have ours. Consider instead the multiple time zones in which humanity lives. It may be morning for me now, but for others it is evening. For me, it may be summer now, but for others it is winter. Time and mortality are relative, not fixed. Likewise, our own mortality is not a bludgeon, a hammer ready to fall, so much as a motion, a movement, a form of being for now, which will be a different form of being later.

Accept, even befriend, your own mortality more deeply every day. At the same time, accept the gift of your life more powerfully every day.

"Creature! I am a creature! I was made for feast. I am built for feast." Pray these words. Meditate these words. Slip into praise as often as possible; it will become gratitude, and you won't find the words *would*, *could*, or *can't* on your lips. They will dissolve into *will* and *can*.

Appreciate time. Be present.

Turn time management into a spiritual activity, one that is about your mortality and your creation, your choice to feast in the midst of famine. In fact, be very careful about using the word *management* in regards to time. Why would time need to be managed? Time needs to be *appreciated*.

I have a friend who never responds either or yes or no when someone asks her to do something that will require a commitment of time. Instead she says, "I'll let you know in three days." She does this as a very intentional, spiritual discipline. She gifts herself with 72 hours to discern what is most important to her. How can she best use her time in a way that nourishes her soul and brings the most meaning to her life and the lives of others?

Someone said to me that she thought most clergy were a mass of "quivering availability," meaning living for others as though they were slaves to their own service. I took that to heart and have learned to say no to *availability* and yes to something like *presence*. Often to be present, I need to be absent. One of the main roads to the land of enough is to withdraw permission from others to tell you what to do with your time.

Just be sure that when you say no to people, you don't say it with negative energy. Say no with Sabbath strength, understanding that you are a person of focus, not fear; a person of choice, not compulsion. Let people know that you are the driver of your life and that you are learning what Kierkegaard means when he says in his famous title, "purity of heart is to will one thing." Use your Sabbath as a discipline to will one thing.

Find a partner

Do none of these things alone. You will fail. Find a time-feast partner and get him or her to help you. Make sure they know your plan to move to feast from famine. Give them permission to challenge you if you fail. Do the same for them. Stay away from people who want to drive your car. Help them drive their own. Steward your energy so that the people around you are with you, not against you. Note that positive energy increases and renews; negative energy depletes and starts whining about how it doesn't have enough time to be different or better.

Don't judge. Forgive yourself. And rejoice.

My nephew Chris stopped thinking about his audiences when he said he was tired of people being so "judgey." That was a good use of a word. We spend so much time being judgey of ourselves. We also worry that people will go judgey *on us*. Withdrawing permission from others to tell you who you are offers a profound release into God's grace and God's kingdom and commonwealth of time. Many call the kingdom of God or the commonwealth of God the *time* of God. That is where we want to live. God tells you who you are – and says you are wonderful. Why bother with other viewpoints?

Remove any sense of blame or shame from yourself or others if you fail and move back to the land of famine. The speed-up is not your fault, nor can you liberate yourself from it alone. Anne Lamott says we are always looking for someone to blame. Instead, why not forgive ourselves and get back on the path of life? Why not make a habit of changing, knowing we will have to change again?

Celebrate this. Rejoice in little steps, a few hours of Sabbath deliverance, a growing sense of freedom in you for feast.

Aim. And don't be afraid to miss.

Finally, after non-participation, after befriending our mortality, after managing our time spiritually and developing a community that will help us, in the land of no-judgement and forgiveness, beyond blame and shame, we return to the question of aim. What are we aiming for and how can it become time feast instead of time famine?

I am always careful about using the word aim because people think it is sneakily judgey. "What if I miss?" they ask. If we overdo our efforts at time feast, we will find ourselves right back in time famine. Less is more. Less is really more, especially because it leads to the time feast. Part of the route to the time feast involves not trying too hard to hit our mark. Grace is our engine and our energy, not works. The system wants us to never fail and to always succeed. The system wants achievement. But we don't *achieve* the time feast. We *live* in it and *appreciate* it. There is a difference. One of the best habits of feasting people is failure. We aren't afraid to fail. We know life is much too important to be taken seriously. We understand failure and know it is the freedom to succeed.

Susan Lewis, an art historian, said that she had "target panic." She studies archery. She went on to say that the secret to personal mastery is to learn to love an "almost hit" or a "near win." The longer we try to become perfect, the longer we will endure target panic and refuse to enjoy what the archer enjoys, which is getting close to where we wanted to be. "Converting success into mastery is learning to appreciate the almost-win," she says. There is no problem in this world that you can't make worse, especially when you spend life over-functioning in order to avoid criticism. There is nothing so perfect as imperfection.

When I talk about aim, I do mean the bull's eye. I also know very few of us will hit our bull's eye. Aim is best when it goes for our personal best, nothing more and nothing less. My son plays a lot of ultimate Frisbee. He even played in a World Ultimate Frisbee Championship in Europe. He was taught by the alternative culture of this game that winning is not the most important thing. What was most important was naming his personal best and aiming for it in each game. When his team lost the world tournament by one point, I was devastated. He was not. He had wanted to make fewer than two turnovers in the game and to throw for three goals. He threw for six and had three turnovers. I'd say he made his goal. I'd say he is more free than I am of the way the systems try to drive us.

Getting Started
(The practice)

1. Carefully assess yourself. How time starved are you? Make a scale from one to five, with five being so serious that your spiritual, mental and physical health are threatened, so much so that you may die prematurely from your lack of nourishment and the presence of stress. Take a personal retreat in which you give yourself a diagnosis. Test it on your best friend. If you find yourself closer to a one than a five, rejoice. Help others achieve your tranquility and ability to feast. If you find yourself closer to a five than a one, get help, starting with your friend. Tell him or her what you intend to do and who you intend to be in a year from now. Calmly plot your resurrection.
2. Assess your spiritual muscles. Are you in good shape? Or do your spiritual muscles suffer from a lack of exercise? Again use a scale of one to five and repeat the above exercise.

3. Begin to untangle and untether from that which is wasting you. Non-participation and re-perception is the direction. List five things that must go. Don't replace them yet. Just let them go. Live empty for a while.
4. Imagine your own death as a beautiful thing. A complete thing. No regrets, just gratitude for living.
5. Begin to aim and to name your aim. Where do you really want to go? Where do you really want to end? Where are you now?
6. Write yourself a letter. Name the moment when you made a turn towards your destination.

Questions for reflection and discussion

1. Let's admit that we are in trouble. Let's not stay in denial but instead talk about how hard it is to get through the day. Say it out loud to your friends. How does the time famine bug and bother you?
2. Moving out of denial is hard. We think we should be stronger, more able. Do you think the time famine is your personal fault? If not, why not? If yes, why?
3. How can we help each other enjoy a time bounty? Are there things we can do to orient each other to feast and to a sense of "enough" time?

Prayer

Please help me become the driver of my own life. Let me not be driven. Let me drive. Amen.

Focus for the Week

Come to terms with your personal diagnosis. How famished are you? How full are you?

CHAPTER TWO
"Real" Technology and Spiritual Technology

Real" technology, as I use the term, has to do with that great miracle the Internet, and spiritual technology has to do with that great miracle "loving engagement." Each *webs*. Each grants us "connectivity." Each allows us to reach out and touch someone. Each is Godly.

Two technologies: how they combine and where they differ

But more and more today, we forget what life was like before the Internet. We forget that you can lovingly engage the world without doing so digitally. People did so for years. In fact, it is good to pause every now and then and remember, if you are old enough, what life was like before your computer or cellphone, Facebook, Twitter, Instagram accounts, or email addresses. If you are too young to remember a time before the capacity to instantly engage in any time zone, don't worry. You can take a history course in the art of the letter and letter-writing; you can learn about a time when notes were carried by horses from one village to another. Read Jane Austen's *Pride and Prejudice* as a great 200-year-old example of horse-carried messages. People connected as richly then as we do now. There were just fewer connections.

There is no doubt that the World Wide Web has contributed to the time famine. Because we *can* connect, we *do* connect, and sometimes we don't know how to disconnect the connect button. More is not necessarily better, even though we have been trained to believe it is.

I think of a thousand religious leaders and firefighters and police responders – "first responders" we call the latter – gathering to greet the pope in the 9–11 museum in downtown Manhattan. It was a powerful day. We had to arrive three hours early in order to clear security. And then we were seated in the bowels of the former World Trade Center to hear the pope sacralize the space and remember the fallen. The fundamental experience of this layered day was the cellphone. Instead of seeing the pope from Row 8, I saw nothing but a cloud of cellphones snapping or recording the entire event. Was this spiritual technology? Yes, in the sense that the thousand present multiplied loving spiritual engagement. No, in the sense that it was very hard to realize where we were, and with *whom* we were, and *who* we were ourselves while there. There was little pause for reflection.

Last fall, a Waterton Canyon park in Colorado decided to close for a time because too many people were taking selfies with bears. And I'll never forget watching the full moon rise through the Eiffel Tower in Paris, while being bombarded by tourists carrying sticks on which they had placed their cellphones for better pictures to send "home." Real technology sometimes steals from us the very time it is trying to record.

There is no need to demonize real technology. There is, however, a need to manage it. We need to put it in its place. A few minutes unrecorded are a great example of time feast.

A sign in the subway said, "Our Apps are so simple that even adults can work them." I love the humour of that because it blesses the child *and* the adult simultaneously. So could technology, but first we have to develop a sense that technology is a tool, like a spoon, which we only use when we are eating. Or a like hoe, which we only use when we are planting. Or a computer, which we only use when we are computing. You don't have to be an environmentalist to wonder about technology. Will it be another thorn in the flesh, another opportunity to hear Thoreau's lament? "Human beings," he said, "have a tendency to become the tools of our tools."

The Digital Revolution has not made false promises so much as we humans have falsely used it, giving it more power than it deserves. There is nothing culturally neutral about technology. It reinforces our sense of progress as a cultural value, which is ecologically dangerous. It confirms the falsehood in us that more is better, which is ecologically dangerous.

Information is one thing, *wisdom* another. Information lets everyone know you were at the Eiffel Tower during a full moon. Wisdom deepens your experience of that moon, such that when you want to tell a loved one or two, not 500, about what the moon means to you, or what France means to you, or what great towers mean to you, you have something to say. Information is the brag: "I was there, then!" Wisdom removes the exclamation points. It may even send a photo to your best friend or the first person you ever went to France with (if you did!) with a kind note and a fond memory, one experienced not just told.

We *can* use all the physical technologies for spiritual purposes, one of which might be an intention to live in time feast instead of time famine. We can send a kind note or a word of encouragement, a poem, or a Tweeted thought, well articulated. We can control our communications so that they do not control us.

Spiritual technologies

John O'Donohue, the late Irish poet, argued that stress results from a misunderstanding of time. We think time is what it isn't. We think of it as a commodity during which we are commanded to rush. Haste is the tool we use on time. "More" has mastered the sense of time in us. Instead, we might imagine time as rhythm, what athletes understand as being in the zone. We know the difference between flow and fast, between haste and the holy. We *do* know, underneath that layer of incarnated cultural instructions, what it means to have our speedometer set on cruise and to be happy cruising.

We don't only commodify time. We don't just misunderstand time and live in the unnecessary stress of that misunderstanding. We also misunderstand the *tools* of making time tender. This is where spiritual technologies come in. I want to redeem the word technology from its "time saving" and efficiency models. I want to point us to some spiritual tools for flow, and rhythm, and tending, and time as our friend.

Worship as a spiritual technology

While this is not a book on worship or liturgy, the relief that true worship brings can never be far away from the time feast. Indeed, worship is a time feast. In worship we sing, pray, listen, recite ancient texts. Feasty and feisty people can also worship in committee meetings or in a street protest or walking a picket line. There is a way to picket and play. The more sense of ritual we put into our everyday life, the more we will get out of our sacralized time. Worship is grotesque when we imagine it as only one time, say Sunday or Saturday. More lovely is having a sense of prayer and pause wherever we are, whenever we are there. That being said, there is nothing like a weekly Sabbath to cohere time and self in a community that has an intention to feast on time. Not easy to find, these ritual observances, once lost, go on to encourage the time famine.

When theologians argue that liturgy is the work of the people, what they mean is that liturgy is our true work. The Westminster Catechism argues that the purpose of the human is to praise God. What better way to praise God than on Sunday or Saturday or Friday, in the company of other people? What better way to tell time what is important to us than to worship and to be part of a worshipping congregation?

If you are a person who thinks you don't have time to worship, watch out. You are obeying the wrong master. You might instead choose to steal some time *from* that master. Non-participation in the master's program might allow you a little time to worship. Your heart will sing. Your voice will pray. You will awaken your inner spiritual muscles. You will learn the art of being mortal. You may even become "beside yourself."

Of course, you may have tried to find a congregation with whom to worship and been unsuccessful. Church or congregation shopping is one of the least satisfying tasks in the world. We want so much from the experience of worship and rarely find it all in one place. I personally worship in three ways. Pentecostal African-American on a Sunday evening, when I can. Episcopal Eucharist at the 8 a.m. slot; and then in my own Baptist/UCC event on Sunday mornings. I get a little of what I need to remain in compliance with the Westminster Catechism from each.

Finding a congregation where you can have a spiritual home can be a daunting task. The best thing I can say is go more than once. Be sure to make at least one friend. Don't expect worship to always be ecstatic or transforming. Understand the quotidian, everydayness, as it applies to worship.

Meditation as a spiritual technology

If you cannot find a congregation, a practice of meditation may be the next best thing for you. Meditation doesn't require a trip to India or even massive instruction. It is, at its heart, a relaxation response, where you simply breathe, focus on your breathing, and do so for as little as a minute at a time. That kind of touchstone keeps you from turning meditation into an Olympic sport, which is one of the sources of the time famine in the first place. Competitiveness is not helpful when it comes to learning spiritual technologies. You are looking for your personal best, not a way to beat out others at something you call a "game."

Many people have turned to Eastern practices in order to fill the void created by so much of mainstream religion, which itself is often caught by the claims of masters other than God. This move towards the Eastern is magnificent in many ways. It can also exoticize the "other" and keep us from the interesting task of reforming our own traditions.

One of the more interesting critiques of meditation and mindfulness practice has to do with the supposed apolitical character of meditative practices. Suzanne Moore, for instance, has criticized mindfulness practices as something like a postmodern opiate for the masses. Cultivating awareness and detachment may, of course, be great for one's mental health, offering a little sanity amidst the constant pressures of day-to-day existence, but for Moore that's the whole problem. She wants us to change the constant pressures of existence, not just find a way out of them for an hour or so a day.

The philosopher and cultural critic Slavoj Žižek has also criticized such practices. Western appropriations of non-Western traditions that emphasize mindfulness, inner peace, disinterest, non-attachment, and so on function, for Žižek, as "the paradigmatic ideology of late capitalism." That is, they "represent the most efficient way for us fully to participate in capitalist dynamics while retaining the appearance of mental sanity." In other words, even something as beautiful as meditation can bend us towards participation in late-stage capitalism.

Mindfulness practices, for Žižek, allow us to have it both ways: we can work and participate in the market more generally without being existentially engaged in such activities, since the latter, in the end, really don't matter for the cultivation of our "inner" selves. It's not what we *do*, but who we are "on the inside" that counts, which is why, for someone like Žižek, the contemporary mindfulness movement is almost perfectly suited for a market society

Counter to Žižek, I would simply point out that we do these things on what we call our own time, a phrase that also shows that much of our time is not really our own. The point of the time feast is to *own* our own time and not be *owned* by our own time.

Meditative practices, in this sense, don't offer us an escape, a way out, but rather an opportunity to engage the world more critically and radically, which is what we need if we are to come to flow within our own time, at work and at play.

The spiritual technology of activism

The most lasting achievement of the United Farm Workers led by Cesar Chavez, that movement that still makes it almost impossible to drink Gallo's wine, was the long-handled hoe. Instead of bending over to hoe, farm workers got a technology that helped their backs last longer.

Called "El Cortito," the old hoe was 24 inches long. It was the single most potent symbol of what was wrong for the farmworkers in California. Chavez and his movement got it banned by the California Supreme Court. It saved backs, which saved spirits, which saved backs.

I was once in jail with the activist and visionary Dorothy Day, during one of these protests for the hoe. I was so excited to be arrested with her only to discover, in the van that took us and five other women away, that she wanted some solitude in jail. "It is the only place I can get it," she said. Dorothy announced to us that she would be meditating and writing until dinner, at which point she would be happy to have some social time with the rest of us. Activists, especially, need "down" time in which to recover from the strain of "up" time battling systems.

I once had to pray in a field in Florida. There was nothing else to do. The demonstration was for the Immokalee Workers. The owner of the tomato field said, "Lady, (I was wearing my collar) you see all those people in the field? I could fire them all right now and in an hour have another 30 to pick these ripe tomatoes." The brutality of his message floored me. We were advocating a raise in price from around $13 a bushel to around $13.40 a bushel, what amounts to pennies on the pound. "If you do that, I'll just fire all of them. I can't get Taco Bell to pay that much for tomatoes." The owner of the field was treating the pickers as if they were not people. He was only thinking about himself. Eventually, there *was* a raise in the price per bushel and Taco Bell paid it. But I had to pray long and hard and get over my fury as well as rejoice in our modest victory.

Many of us go deep into the time famine because we can't stand injustice. We become so active as activists that we fail to manage our furies. We work on fumes. The main time for prayer or meditation is when you are in highest motion.

Scripture as a spiritual technology

While the story of the workers in the vineyard (Matthew 20:1–16) is not about farm workers, it is also exactly about farm workers. Here Jesus undermines the entire concept of wage work. You come early, you get paid for the whole day. You come late, you get paid for the whole day. Jesus is saying something important here about how wages and work need to be much less connected. He is, after all, a Utopian. He is also talking about repentance, and saying that it is never too late for the Almighty to give you a big break.

The story is likewise about spiritual punctuality. Spiritual punctuality is very different from punching a clock. Spiritual punctuality converses with time about its direction and its aim and its point. Is justice being served? Or are we just standing around waiting for our next paycheque or vacation? Is our life vocation and coherence being served? Or are we on hold till something like "us" or "our life" can happen? It is never too late for Spirit to move in on you, even if you are working in a field.

Again, let's look at the language. "Punching the clock?" Why? Are you mad at the clock? Yes, most of us are mad at the clock. We think of it as our dominatrix, not our friend. Here I need to digress and say a few things about the meaning of work, all based in this terribly important scripture about work.

Of course work is about wages. I believe that in our reduced 21st-century state, where work has been largely reduced to its rewards, I could just stop here and advocate a living wage, a reduction in the disproportion, where some get a lot of money for moving their money around while others get a little money for hard labour. The radical economists at Mondragon, a huge cooperative movement founded in Spain, argue that the best change of all would be to make the highest paid person in an organization only able to make 100 times more than the lowest paid person. Again, that Utopian idea probably won't happen any time soon. Thus we are stuck with books like this one to help us through till the great day comes.

Our wage arrangements are simply wrong, especially if you look at domestic workers, care of seniors, care of children, and school teaching. You can do much better in the world of finance.

Jesus was addressing the physical and spiritual problem of bending over to work. Or bending down to work. Or not having the right technology or ideas about work in the first place.

So I ask you: Do you work for money or for meaning or for

both? Is the meaning of life getting enough money during the week so that you can have leisure on the weekend? Or is the meaning of leisure on the weekend getting you strong enough to work during the week for the money? Or is work a kind of circle, meant to exist between your labour and the grapes of wine, not the grapes of wrath? I love when the aging dowager in the show *Downton Abbey* asks her leisure-class question: "What is a weekend?"

God knows the meaning of work has taken more than a few hits lately. "At an ideological level, contemporary work does not function on the basis of a gap between participation and engagement, between our work and our 'inner selves.'" Rather, the whole point of work in late capitalism is, as Frédéric Lordon has argued, to close this gap, to force an identification of the whole self with the desires of one's employer. That is, one *must* be internally motivated toward and existentially engaged in one's work – or else face the consequences. Work is not just something we do but who we *are* – which is why we must be "collegial," "team players," "share the values" of our employer, and be committed to "the future of the company."

That is a far cry from the Utopian dream of the Haymarket rioters. In 1886, the Haymarket protestors advocated eight hours for work, eight hours for sleep, and eight hours for what we will. Twenty thousand people took to the streets in Chicago. The incident that caused the demonstration was the killing, by police, of four workers at the McCormick Reaper works. Interesting, right? Never imagine that state violence will not erupt to keep workers under control. Never underestimate how insurrectionary it is to live according to the time feast, not the time famine, or to use the right kind of hoe for your back.

Spiritual technology joins real technology to help us have revolutions today, revolutions that are internal to us, as we keep ritual right alongside. Tiananmen Square could never have happened without real technology. Spiritual technology is our aim and our intention, ritualized in whatever field or office we find ourselves, even if we have to sneak our way to it when the boss is not looking. Real technology is "just" a tool to help us feast on the gift of time. When we abuse it, we lose its gift. When we use it, we realize its gift.

Spiritual leisure

Work's relationship to money affects just about everything. It even affects our leisure pursuits, like travel. The monetization of just about everything infects not just working practices but even such supposed pleasures as tourism. The biggest complaint I hear from my friends who travel a lot: beggars asking us for money. Then again I'll never forget one of my fellow travellers in China taking a picture of a girl as she gave her some money. That one went in her scrapbook. Instead of feasting on time, on her vacation, she was trying to impress someone else. She was not whole where she was, but still reaching for more of what she has already been given as a child of God. "More" was ruining her vacation, the way it also ruins our lives.

In contrast, I offer you the work that one child did to make money near Machu Picchu. At first it was sheer delight to watch that girl whom everybody thought was a boy. She was running with abandon, in a kind of flow. When she caught the bus at the bottom, she had a group of helpers ready to receive the tips we offered for our enjoyment of her race. She was having fun making money from our leisure. Why not? There is nothing wrong with or about money. What is wrong is the way we grind our spirits to the bone making it.

Consider instead the arts of spiritual leisure, of being willing to enjoy yourself at work, even if your work is a kind of interesting begging. There is delight in a girl chasing a bus down a long mountain road. There is beauty in the farm work of the long-handled hoe, where we dig deeply enough into our experience to know what the meaning of work is for us. Imagine meditation practices that engage us in genuine detachment from the penny-more-a-pound we need to pay for tomatoes. Imagine freedom from the famine for the feast.

People who call themselves "bioneers" head for wellness on several fronts. They want to work *for* wellness, *at* wellness, *in* wellness. My little vision of Utopia has always had everybody working physically *and* spiritually – a little bit of each. I'd love to touch more soil and fewer computer keys. Most people would, I suspect. Except maybe for those people who never get to touch a computer key. In the time feast, everybody would have a kind of work that activated his or her mind and body and spirit. Until that time comes, some will remain the "head" of the world and others will remain "the feet," and *all* will suffer needlessly. Some will be treated only as brains and others will be treated only as bodies, and both bodies and minds will suffer. Isn't it odd that some people go the gym to keep their muscles alive, that they *pay* for exercise, while others don't need to, so exhausted are they by the sweat on their brow that they don't need to purchase more?

We who are bent over our computers can learn from the girl who knew how to dance down the hill. We can learn from the activism of not accepting that "things the way they are" *need* to be the way they are. Whenever anyone says to you "that's just the way it is," you can quietly suggest to him or her that it need not be so. Such activism is quiet and tender. It comes from a spirit that knows how to feast. It comes from spiritual leisure, which we can experience while travelling, at home, at work, and at rest. Spiritual leisure is not just a weekend pursuit.

Conclusion

"Real" technology and "spiritual" technology are two sides of the same coin, which is you. They are not opposites, but blends. They blend best by people who aim for feast and don't accept the orders of the masters, even the internalized ones who use their tools so well upon us. Our masters don't blend. They stay separate and they cut us off from each other, and ourselves when we imagine tools as ends not means of life. Spiritual technology is the end, the living of life from the inside out. Material technology is one means we can use to evoke the inner power to master the outer destination.

Questions for reflection and discussion

1. My favourite tool is a scissors. I love to clip things and give articles to people. I love to cut out pictures of things I like and keep them on my desk until I don't find them fascinating anymore. My favourite picture is a tree house. My second favourite is a cat sleeping in a bird feeder. My third favourite

is a cat sleeping in a mailbox. Without my scissors, I could not adorn the place where I do most of my work, my desk. With the scissors, I can make it beautiful. What is your favourite tool? Why?
2. How do you balance physical and mental work in your work? Which way would you like most to rebalance, if at all?
3. What do you do for spiritual leisure? Is it something that you pay for, or something that takes you out of the money-for-pleasure economy? What "low-cost form of personal entertainment," like taking a walk or biking to church on Sunday, could you learn?
4. With whom do you worship? If you don't worship, why not? If you do, what's missing in your worship habit? What is best about your worship habit?
5. Give your computer a name. Is it a fun name or a mean name? Do you like your computer or your cell phone? What do you like about them? What don't you like about them? How would your rate yourself as a user of technology? Are you helped or hurt by technology? Give yourself a technology grade. An "A" is for someone who *uses* technology as well as others use a scissors or a hoe. An "F" is for someone who is *used by* technology.
6. What help can we give each other to keep technology from mastering us instead of us mastering it? Support groups for phone abusers? Repeat after me: Nobody makes me Tweet, or spend time on Facebook, or LinkedIn, except me.

Prayer

Tame me and my tools, O God. Let me use them well, so well that I learn to lovingly engage what I can lovingly engage, no more and no less.

Focus for the week

Imagine that you have all the money you need. How would you spend your days? How much of this fantasy can you import into your "real" life?

CHAPTER THREE

The Work-Family Dilemma

Sigmund Freud argued that life has two fundamental meanings: work and love. I think he was right, but putting those two together has become more than a little difficult for many of us. Many people sacrifice themselves and their own inner life in order to make "ends" meet. By ends we usually mean two things: the end or point of the matter, and the time between when our money runs out and the end of the month. Many people also mean it when they say, "My house is a mess." Very few people feel "cohered," as in *integrated*, as in *whole*, as in *spiritually and managerially in charge of their own life*. Full integration of self with life is probably not possible – but much more coherence is possible than many imagine.

The goal of this chapter is to get us to the point where we can say "My house is my home. I live well there." The other goal is to say, "My work is my vocation. I choose to do it." To learn to work and to be at home – in this world, not the next – requires everything that we said in the first chapter plus some savvy, canny approaches to real life. Learning to love, whether in a family or in a community, will take all the spiritual skill you have, and then some. Learning to work isn't any easier. Work has a way of making you work. We also know that family has a way of suffering when there is *too* much work. It's complicated. And it's very hard to tell your boss, even if *you* are the boss, that you don't feel like working today. Coherence requires the integrity of work and home, family and job, self and its obligations.

Re-imagining our aim in life

Someone asked my grandson what he wanted to be when he grows up. He said, "A daddy." I was thrilled with that answer, for two reasons. First, he somehow had become free of the doctor, lawyer, fireman, Indian-chief world in which most men used to grow up. New possibilities have opened up for him. Second, in the past we were supposed to *be* our work. We were *defined* by our work. What is it that you want *be*? That world is changing!

An even better answer to the question "What do you want to be when you grow up?" might be, "I want to be cohered by God in work and at home." I like to think that is the next generation's answer. Ideally, we might imagine work and family as a systemic choice cohered by the one we know as God.

Of course, God is not easily defined here. Permit me, then, to continue to use the word God for that which is larger than you, that which created you, that which "cores" you? If you can't grant that permission, I do understand. Just make sure there is *something* larger than you so that you don't end up whining in existential aloneness, "It's all up to me." *That* is not coherence. That is loneliness. That is a false read of the world. If it is all up to you, it is probably because you have consented to be a victim of unjust workplaces and an unjust world. If it is all up to you, you have probably failed to love enough to be loved. Yes, that's how you find love. You love.

Our "scripts" and coherence

Coherence comes through the exegesis of our life and our time. Exegesis is a fancy word for perception or interpretation. If we perceive time as the conflict between our obligations in work and our obligations to family, we are probably going to feel that life is a tightrope. Or a double-dutch jump skipping game. The rope swings and we jump over it. The tightrope requires a constant balancing. We rarely relax. Re-perceiving life as both long and short, as both eternal and limited to the number of our own days, as God-given as opposed to human-made, can give us the rhythm we need to jump rope and have fun doing it, or to walk the tightrope like a pro.

The practical and spiritual question of interpretation is whether you can think something through or does it think *you* through. How active can we even be in interpretation? Or is interpretation a passive activity, like being scripted for life by things that happened long ago?

The word *scripture* has its root in the word script or scribe. It is that which is written down. Today, I'm told, people don't talk about being scripted so much as they talk about the narrative that has formed them, the frame that framed them, the story in which they live. More often than not, we talk about being scripted as a negative thing. I was scripted, some say, to become the alcoholic that I am. Or I am scripted, some say, to not trust men. Or women. Or dogs. We use the language of being written upon as a kind of curse. When we say we are scripted, we imagine we can't deviate very much from our "instructions."

Scripture, scripted words, can also be a blessing. They can frame and hold us, as this text argues: "For the word of God is alive and active. Sharper than any double-edged sword, it penetrates even to dividing soul and spirit, joints and marrow; it judges the thoughts and attitudes of the heart" (Hebrews 4:12). This is a fat text, a meaty text, warning us not to be literal about scripture or the larger scripts that our forebears have recorded for our instruction. The word of God is alive and active, not dead or static. It is also sharp and can cut. It can cut by the way you try to make it dead, as some who defend the Koran are doing, inappropriately and wrongly. It can cut by the way you try to make it living, only to your century or your seminary or your moment in time. You can get stuck in the script of your day and not understand what Karl Barth argued – that indeed scripture is such a profound disturbance that it will need constant, daily demythologizing in order to penetrate to its purpose. Its purpose is to ground you in a unified soul and body, an integrated human, one who is grounded in the big written-down truths and is able to transcend them.

Note that in this one verse we are warned not to separate our soul from our body, our joints from our spirit, and our spirits from our marrow. We are also warned not to be static in our interpretation of our work or family, vocation or intimacy. Finally, scripture is a judge, an exegete, and an interpreter. Indeed it judges the thoughts and attitudes of the heart. You are active, not passive, in interpretation of your own life.

So of course we are scripted. Our scripts can be a blessing, or they can be a curse. When I speak of coherence as a script we write on our own hearts, I mean the blessing of living large, in feast, instead of in famine. Only *you* can know the specifics of your own "job description." In the next chapter, I will talk more about that. For now, begin to experience the permission to choose a script, perhaps a scripture, by which to interpret your life.

Ancient testimonies

Consider these additional scriptures, these "scripts," as rendered in the *Common English Bible*, as God's point of view on time. At a minimum, they will expand your horizon of time and show you a path out of the hurtful intensity of a day-by-day-by-day-by-day time famine. They promise a way out, a way forward, a way to be large, no matter how serious your time famine is.

2 Peter 3:8 – Don't let it escape your notice, dear friends, that with the Lord a single day is like a thousand years and a thousand years are like a single day.

Proverbs 16:9 – People plan their path, but [God] secures their steps.

Psalm 90:12 – Teach us to number our days so we can have a wise heart.

Jeremiah 29:11 – I know the plans I have in mind for you, declares [God]; they are plans for peace, not disaster, to give you a future filled with hope.

Ephesians 1:10 – This is what God planned for the climax of all times: to bring all things together in Christ, the things in heaven along with the things on earth.

2 Corinthians 6:1–2 – Since we work together with him, we are also begging you not to receive the grace of God in vain. He says, *I listened to you at the right time, and I helped you on the day of salvation.* Look, now is the right time! Look, now is the day of salvation!

Mark 13:32 – But nobody knows when that day or hour will come, not the angels in heaven and not the Son. Only [God] knows.

Psalm 31:15 – My future is in your hands. Don't hand me over to my enemies, to all who are out to get me!

Philippians 3:13–14 – Brothers and sisters, I myself don't think I've reached it, but I do this one thing: I forget about the things behind me and reach out for the things ahead of me. The goal I pursue is the prize of God's upward call in Christ Jesus.

James 4:14 – You don't really know about tomorrow. What is your life? You are a mist that appears for only a short while before it vanishes.

Psalm 90:2 – Before the mountains were born, before you birthed the earth and the inhabited world – from forever in the past to forever in the future, you are God.

Psalm 90:4 – because in your perspective a thousand years are like yesterday past, like a short period during the night watch.

Proverbs 16:3 – Commit your work to [God], and your plans will succeed.

Ephesians 5:16 – Take advantage of every opportunity because these are evil times.

These passages on time are great starting points for coherence. They show a guiding principle for time and move us out of the "work-family" struggle, which many of us live in during the famine. They enlarge time, and that enlargement enlarges us. Instead of managing time as the inevitable tension between work and family, we see time management as the spiritual skill of living wisely in the largeness of our creation.

Demythologizing our scripts

Whenever we interpret anything, we have to be careful and conscious about our own myths. We all have them. They are the curse aspect of being scripted. Learning our scripts and *unlearning some of them* is key to coherence.

Demythologizing is even better than re-perceiving or exegeting or interpreting. Demythologizing involves a highly encouraged suspicion that is based in the experience of grace. The great theologian Karl Barth argued that the only decent basis for human integrity – the companionship of body and mind, spirit and mind, marrow and mind – is piety. Yup, piety. What is piety? Piety is nothing more or less than religious feeling, our sense of absolute dependence on that which we are *not*, and cannot be. It is the feeling of the presence of God. In other words, for many of us, right next to most of our scripts (all those ideas that are constantly having absurd conversations in our heads) lies a desire for a sense of connection – perhaps even deep, intimate connection – to something larger, more cosmically meaningful than we sense our own small lives to be. Some call this "something" God, others Jesus. The names are myriad.

When it comes to the time famine, we have to find a theology that will pull us back from the brink of utilitarianism. Liberal theology didn't become liberation theology because it froze God in a book. Rather, it warmed the heart.

At the same time, a good theology, a good "story" around which to orient our life, will also *challenge* our heart. The gospel, to Barth and to me, is the shattering disturbance that brings everything into question. It is both the sacrifice and the cosmic event of Jesus. We don't have to believe in Christian supremacy in order to imagine the cosmic event of Jesus as disturbing. It may mean that the ways we live, so colonized by the powers that be, are not the best ways to live – that instead of bowing down we could be lifted up. These are big ideas and powerful enough to work against the oppressive time famine to which we consent.

Small examples are necessary, otherwise you won't be threatened enough, or encouraged enough, to care about scripture. You will remain in spiritual unconsciousness about what really matters. You will live an uncohered life.

Let's warm up to the small by thinking about the act of journalling. When we write something down, it's often because it matters. When you write it down, it makes a difference. Something happens in the writing down. Sarah Manguso's memoir *Ongoingness* argues that we keep a diary when we find ourselves in moments too full. We keep journals to be able to say we were really paying attention. Journalling is a strong defence against waking up and finding that you've missed life.

Journalling is one example of inner scaffolding. It is similar to scheduling a day, which adds to scheduling a *way* – a *way* to *be* in time. Our calendars tell us a lot about our lives. Thus, they are a good interpretive device. They tell us what is important to us and what is not, what is necessary and what is not. Often our days and our diaries, our journals, our calendars, are filled with the quest for what really matters. We write our scripts, our personal scripture this way, that living word of God *in us*. We *listen* for the word of God and then we *live* from it, towards our daily lives in work and family.

Many people love their work and see in it a vocation. Many more don't. For the majority of people, work is something you do for money. How can we aim to be a human *being* while also knowing we have to be a human *doing*? That is my question here. If life demands that you work eight hours a day on a job that is not a vocation, and it takes two hours a day to get there, how do you find a way to live in the few hours you have left? How do you keep your spiritual muscles alive while your material muscles are being overworked? How do you love a family or a companion or a best friend or even a dog or cat, when you are exhausted physically, mentally and spiritually by work? Only by a power larger than yourself.

I like to ask people what wage they think should be paid for living. Often the answers are very surprising. A little freedom. A little relaxation. A day or so that is mine every now and then. A kind word. A thank you. A little respect. When we get too deeply into the definition of time as working at work and working at home, we become as small as that definition. Time feast comes when we enlarge our perception of time, and of ourselves.

Techniques for time management

Time management techniques will not take you all the way to feasting, but without them you will have a much longer journey. These techniques come from the experience of grace. They do not create grace. They are responses to the interpretation and perception of grace. Let's consider half a dozen examples of time management techniques.

1. Discipline your computer lest it discipline you.
2. Take time off. Taxi drivers are my best teachers. Many quit at 3 p.m. In New York City, where I live, it is almost impossible to get a cab at 3 p.m., because the drivers are all heading home. Sometimes they'll pick you up if you are going their way. They also drive five days a week. I will never know why so many people think they aren't worth a day off.
3. Make sure you have a date night, if partnered, or a community night, if single. Do something beautiful with yourself for yourself, even if you don't have any money. Go sit in a park.
4. If you have children, rotate trips or outings or something with them as individuals, not en masse. You'll be amazed at how much more you will enjoy them when they are out of sibling rivalry mode. I took my kids on train trips around the country, one child each year. They were the best times of our lives.
5. Sleep eight hours a night. Imagine that you deserve to be well rested.
6. Learn the art of conflict management or community organizing if you have a mean boss. You deserve justice in the workplace.

Suffer — *gracefully*

I do not intend to offer illusory hopes here. Some jobs and some relationships just have to be endured. You may have a family in which one member has a chronic illness. You may have a family in which one member is seriously addicted or mentally ill. You may work in a grocery store and not in a farm market. You may work for a mega-corporation when what you really want to do is artisanal craft. You may honour the work of the plumber as much as that of the poet, but feel stuck in a dry-cleaning business. You may have what I have, which is enormous peasant envy. And there may be very little you can do to change your circumstances at this point in your life. If that is true of you, or about you or your situation, ignore these six techniques. Or try to change what you are now trying to endure. But make a decision to suffer. Don't suffer out of helplessness. Suffer because you understand that suffering is what you have to do. Victims suffer pointlessly. Victors suffer for a point or a purpose or a reason. Suffer with as much grace as you have when joyful and cohered.

Create a theology, a big picture for your time

More importantly create a theology – a way to think about God that is simple enough to be true for you – a "big picture," for your time-management techniques. Make your story clear and real. What is the role of God or Spirit in your story? Note I just listed six techniques. There are many more and you can read hundreds of books about how to manage your time. I want to teach you more about *why* than *how* to manage your time. Why? Because you are worth it. Because you belong to God and to yourself. Because you deserve the wages you want – in both money and appreciation and respect. Why? Because of grace and God's intention for you to live in grace.

I loved the single woman who rented a place in our house after our kids were gone. She was an Italian filmmaker and had two kids. She bathed and dressed them every night in their school clothes so that she didn't have to dress them again in the morning. She believed enough in her work to cherish and protect her time. She also loved her children and had the most stylish outfits – half pajamas, half sweat pants, all cotton. She had a management strategy as well as theology for time. Again, by theology I mean she way of thinking about what mattered most to her. Theology is very personal; it is the way we get to our core and get basic about what matters most to us. Often, we call that which matters most to us "God."

Changing our scripts from famine to feast

Let me repeat some oft-heard phrases and then translate them from famine to feast. You can do a lot to cohere your life by catching yourself in clichés like these. When you catch yourself, make your own translation. *Re-perceive* what you are saying. Take an ancient text or scripture and quarrel with your own clichés. Learn how to live cohered by practicing on your own language.

1. **"Running late."** What does it mean to run all the time and still be late? What is "on time" for you?
2. **"Running on fumes."** Running on fuel that fuels and renews me.
3. **"Burnt out."** Human beings are not machines, we regenerate by giving ourselves away.
4. **"Don't have enough time."** Eternity is a frame.
5. **"Got wasted."** Got used.
6. **"I'm driving myself crazy."** Why not drive yourself well? Who is driving who anyway?
7. **"She's driving me crazy."** Why the word drive?
8. **"I'm in the fast lane."** Why? Where are you going?
9. **"Your active life in your senior years."** What if in my senior years I want to sit in a rocker? "Be still and know that I am God."
10. **"Workaholic." "Multi-tasking."** Awake, awake to love and work.

When you learn how to listen to what you are saying, and to interpret it, you will find yourself gradually changing towards a more cohered life.

Conclusion

Malcolm Gladwell's book *Outliers: The Story of Success* discloses quite brilliantly the way most of us depend way too much on our peers. Successful people break this pattern. We think for ourselves. We think outside the proverbial box. We distrust the conventional wisdom.

So I ask again, can you think something through or does it think you through? Did your superb liberal arts education or Sunday school work or not? When was the last time you changed your mind about something? Like the "correct" way to talk about terrorism, so much of which is rooted in the protection of ancient scripts? Or the "correct" way to talk about how you spend your days, liberally scripted to be against the monetization of just about everything, but imagining *falsely* that there isn't anything you can do about it anyway?

Rev. Otis Moss, the pastor of Trinity Church in Chicago, accuses most of us of sanitizing our scripted stories. He says he woke up one day and took a good long look at his teenagers and realized he was raising a thug and a thuggette. Ouch. Many parents, and I am one, have woken up years later only to realize the hard way that we missed a lot of marks in how we loved the children we assured ourselves we loved so thoroughly. It doesn't matter that "they turned out all right," or some other cliché we use to massage our failures. What matters is what we didn't see when we could have seen it, had we the freedom to look and see.

Joan Didion calls our masters "the Himalayas of tedium." I know most of us would like to blame the big colonizers of capitalism and literalism. We might blame instead our tedious participation in their calendars, their assumptions about our days.

I ask again, have you changed your mind about anything lately? Or in the last year? If not, why not? Wouldn't a constant practice of demythologizing be a blessing to your life, maybe not immediately, but on that day when you wake up and look back and say "Oh my, how could I have missed that?"

To cohere a life you must write your own script, slowly, carefully and meaningfully.

Questions for reflection and discussion
1. When did you last experience grace? What was it like?
2. Which of the scriptures warms you or speaks to you most directly?
3. Which of the clichés do you use the most? Why?
4. Which of the words of transition do you like the most: exegesis, reimagining, re-perceiving, re-interpreting, demythologizing? Do you have a different transition word? What is it?
5. When was the last time you changed your mind?

Prayer
Frame me for feast, O God. Reframe me, again and again.

Focus for the week
Remember a place and a time when you truly changed. Was it from inner strength or outer push, or both?

CHAPTER FOUR

A Recipe for Feast
WRITING YOUR PERSONAL COHERENCE

In the first chapter, we talked about measuring your own personal time famine. How difficult is your situation? In the second chapter, we talked about so-called "real" technologies and spiritual technologies: how they differ and how they can complement each other. In the third chapter we talked about the work-family dilemma, how many people have difficulty cohering love and work, family and jobs, self and others. In each chapter, the antidotes for the trouble involved non-participation in the systems that hurt you, or what I am calling the refusal to be a victim or to be driven. Be a victor, be a driver, not a driven victim. After all, it is *your* life and *your* time that is at stake.

In Chapter Three we also talked about beginning to write a script for yourself that involved some answer to the question of what God wants from you. I admitted that knowing that is hard. Even harder is knowing who or what God is. Yes, I assume some kind of personal God, some kind of reason for your particular set of genomic material, some answer to the question of *why* you are here. You don't have to go all the way to the kind of God expressed in the Bible, the one who counts the hairs on your head. You don't have to believe in a fate or a destiny or a destination for yourself. Even if you only manage your script as a metaphor and refuse to take it literally, you can still broach the subject of *why you*.

The *why* of you

Here we take a crack at answering the question, *"Why you?"* If you really think you are here to cure cancer, get going. If you really think you are here to stop war, get cracking. If you really think there is no reason for you being here, then let yourself be pushed around by internalized capitalism, or shame and blame. There is no reason not to. Since there is no positive *why* for you, you may as well stick with the negative *whys*. You might even avoid the time famine with that answer. Why bother doing *anything* if there is no reason for you?

Most of us get stranded some place in between the heroic answer and the non-answer. We find it so difficult to believe that we matter that even humility doesn't serve us. We become the kind of nihilist for whom it is easy to be in a world where human life is so frequently devalued. That nihilist isn't even really afraid of life, or mortality either. There are benefits to not pushing the *why* of you. You don't really fear death because life isn't that important to you. And you don't really have a time famine because whatever you do with what Mary Oliver calls your "one precious life" is just fine.

The other pole in the meaning-nothingness polarity is the heroic one. Here we justify our lives with something splendid. Mozart comes to mind, or Keats or Einstein or King. We are driven to achieve what grabs us by the lapel and shakes us so deeply that we cannot *not* do it. This kind of heroism also gets us out of the time famine. As long as we are composing, we are doing the right thing. We are in our groove or zone.

But most of us are neither heroic nor nihilist. We're the ones who skip the double-dutch rope. We don't want to die uncohered or unfulfilled. Nor do we want to live driven lives. We want to approach our meaning by knowing what it is, and by having a stake in accomplishing most of it.

What will make this work easy is our ability to be normal. Normal people sort of "get" where they are going some of the time. Normal people are usually very humble and "down-to-earth," that great phrase that means just what it says. *Humus*, or earth, is the root of the word humble. Normal people normalize themselves and each other. We find value in grace, not works; in grace, not achievement; in gladness at having our genome, but not prideful gladness. Just plain old gladness, the kind that lets you be happy to be alive, as long as the masters who want to use you and use you up aren't driving you. Normal people give themselves permission to have a simple vision, and to know what it is, and to try to live by it. Normal people are neither hyperconnected the way many who live for the approval of others are, nor are we hyper-disconnected the way people who can't figure out how to care for anything or anyone are. We avoid the *hyper-* and the *dis-* and just get connected. We connect to our work, which we choose. We connect to our loved ones, whom we choose. We connect normally, neither for approval nor for money, but because we *choose* to connect. Our vision is so normal that it can be very small. We can be happy very small because the big stuff – the grace that tells you that you don't have to prove yourself – is taken care of. We aren't justifying ourselves. We are justified.

Question your past, and your present

Before you develop your own coherence in some kind of life mission statement or poem or koan or word or gesture, answer a few questions. Answer them in the quiet of your own heart. You may choose to tell someone you love, but as your beginning answer them only to yourself.

Delve into your childhood. Who did your parents think you were? Many immigrants like me lived to assure our parents that they had made a good decision coming to the new world. We were here to salve their broken hearts at having to leave home. We were here to "better" them, and to justify their flight. Many of us, immigrant or not, had the script of upward mobility written straight on our heart. We were only good if we did *better*. Much of the time famine has its source in the directives towards *more* and *better*, which define upward mobility. We keep trying to achieve in order to realize the script written upon our hearts. For most people, that upward mobility, even when achieved, takes a large toll. It distances us from feasting in time, and it distances us from our parents. Often we have to give up that script in order to do what our parents thought they wanted for us. Your childhood may be neither of these two scripts. Find out what it is and ask yourself, as an adult, is this what you still want? Or better, is the cost of the script worth the price you are paying for it? Even better, what *is* the cost of this script? And does it have the ping of God to it? Is this what God wants for you?

The older you get, the more able you will be to name this early script. It may be one that you love and that is just right for you. You may be one of those lucky people who were told early to live the life you choose. Maybe you were alerted to the grace of God so deeply that you never forgot you are a child of God and your parents. On the other hand, you may be one of those more normal people who weren't parented as well as you would have wished to be, or even as well as your *parents* wished you to be. You may find in older age that you are kicking up all the dust of childhood. You will surely know what that dust is and be able to name it.

Delve into your workplace. What is its script for you? Is it vocational? Or avocational? By *vocation* I mean that which you were created or intended to do. Vocation is your call from the one you know as God, or if not God, from holy forces larger than yourself. By *avocation* I mean the things that cause you praise and joy. Some people work without vocation but *do* find a call in something that is not full time, but instead fulfills time for them. Are your vocations and avocations Godly? Must you stay at the job you are in, even if it is not *vocational* for you? What can you give your work that you are not already giving it? What will the cost be to your family, or your love life, or your health if you work harder? Do you experience time famine or feast at work?

Delve into your love life and your family life. Is it satisfying? Is it more grace or more obligation? Is it what you wanted it to be? Is it what your family of origin wanted for you? What could you do to feast more at home? What could you do to lessen famine at home?

Begin to draw the patterns in your script of origin and your script at work and at home. Are there congruencies? Are there patterns that satisfy and dissatisfy you? For what can you dare to aim, based on what you know about yourself? What spiritual muscles will you need in order to take aim? Remember: success is not a bull's eye. Success is aiming, and one near miss after another. There is a difference between achieving success and knowing where you want to go.

In the time famine, as Stephen Covey demonstrates so ably in his marvellous book *The 7 Habits of Highly Successful People*, arguably the best book on writing a personal mission statement there is, most of us are stranded between the *urgent* and the *immediate*, and never get to the *important* matters of our lives. The reason is that we often obey the masters we think are hidden in work and family, and never get to master ourselves. Coherence is self-mastery and self-direction. Incoherence is letting the masters rule. Covey says that if you find yourself at the end of too many days wondering why you never got to do what you wanted to do, start every day doing the *important* thing that you wanted to do. You will discover less of the urgent and more of the important every day that you operate *first* from your mission and second from your obligations. You begin naming the masters. You end mastering the masters. When you master the masters, the first thing you do every day involves mastery. The last thing you do every day involves obligation. You begin to feast on time.

Some sample mission statements

I am a big fan of Eileen Fischer clothing and an even bigger fan of their mission statement as a company. In Eileen Fischer VISION 2020, the company says the following:

> No excuses. Our vision is for an industry where human rights and sustainability are not the effect of a particular initiative but the cause of a business well run. Where social and environmental injustices are not unfortunate outcomes but reasons to do things differently. Where excuses are ignored and action is taken. We're working toward a world in which the clothes you love to wear create nothing but love.

The clarity and pugnacity of this statement delights me. Clothing is the point, but below the point is a process that does not degrade the environment or the people who work in the business. I particularly like the idea of no excuses. Who needs excuses if they are a child of God's grace? Who needs excuses for consenting to be hurt, or to live in the time famine?

I am conflicted with two different mission statements for myself right now. One is that I want to score a ten on the dismount, which is to say that I think of retirement as an Olympic sport. I source most of the time famine I still experience right here. I want to leave my church in such good shape – to the point of raising the money for a new roof as my underground goal – that no one can fault me about its future. I love the church very, very much. I love what it is doing. I am also ego driven, like David with Goliath, and ridiculously afraid of failure.

A friend became a little God to me when she said, "Donna, you can't secure the future of this church with a new roof. No one has ever been able to secure us. We are destined to live in danger, as an urban church with a big mission. Get over it. Just figure out what you want to do before you retire, and retire. And make sure you keep loving us."

I am so afraid of being a tugboat without a barge that I drive myself *to* and *through* time famine. I do too much. I overfunction. Like way too many pastors, I overfunction in such a way that I actually infantilize lay people. I witness to how good it is to work hard instead of what I really want to do, in my coherence, which is to show how great *God* is. I can show you (and so can my therapists) where this comes from in my childhood, where it comes from in the way ministry is practiced today, in internalized capitalism and in distance from grace. Don't worry, I won't bore you with these details.

I can also tell you that a mightier coherence for me is the more humble one. I have a mission statement that is much more useful. I got it during a workshop with Stephen Covey: "I am on earth to provide spiritual nurture for public capacity." I will have become my intended self by spiritually nurturing my congregants and my husband and my children and my friends in such a way that they are more capable for public life, less the victim of the time famine, and more the driver of their own life, in community with others. Other clergy are to do other things. Some have the gift of healing. Some have the gift of the sacrament or of the spoken word. I have the gift of nurture, and the gift to teach and elicit public capacity.

How do I know when I am succeeding? When my community and family are more able for the life they choose. Does it matter how many people I nurture for public capacity? Yes. More is better. And no, too much is too much. That's why I need to be the kind of leader who creates other leaders who do what I do. My "product" is capable, well-fed people. I am most coherent and alive when my work punches both the "personal" button and the "public" button. An example would be working with undocumented immigrants, or with leaders of social movements, or with innovators. My metric is in constant motion because I tend to err on the side of more being better – and brag about growing congregations – rather than keeping my David and Goliath straight.

Our church has *two* statements, which we use again and again to show why we think we are here. First, we are a "church that is a little bit different that wants to make a big difference." I like the way its mission and my mission weave in and out of each other. The other statement is that we are "open in so many ways." Judson Memorial is a rogue congregation, always working as the Research and Development arm for the wider progressive church. Being Baptist and United Church of Christ, we believe in a rooted and communal soul freedom, one that disdains just about every kind of censorship, both public and private, internal and external. Our biggest challenge is realizing that we are actually a very *normal* congregation, with all the ups and downs and ins and outs of every other congregation, progressive or not, rogue or not, big or little. We have an awful time with the conceit of "exceptionalism." So do I. We are a good match.

As Etsy.com transitions to a new offspring, Etsy.org, a new mission statement was needed. It needed to be different than and similar to the parent mission. Etsy.org is a new child of Etsy.com, the very successful online platform that helps people to sell their arts and crafts. Etsy.org teaches people how to be spiritual entrepreneurs and how to link their avocation to their vocation. Regenerative leadership is the strategy we need for mission coherence. A secondary aspect of this new venture is helping people make money at what they love to do, rather than at what they *have* to do. I am involved as one of the teachers. I teach the spiritual side of business development. We came up with the following:

> Our mission is to educate entrepreneurs in ways that develop the human capacity, convey the wisdom, evoke the insights, and foster the community needed to build regenerative businesses.

Developing your mission statement

Most people find it very difficult to boil down their personal or organizational or family mission statement to one sentence. We know how much we want to jam into it. We also know how a fat mission statement leads to an unfocused life, one where way too many masters call your name and you never really know how to declare completion or coherence.

Plus, we are aware of many forms of sneaky taxation during the time famine. We don't really have an hour; we have that hour minus the tax of checking our email, our texts, our Facebook, our Instagrams, and returning our phone calls. That takes at least ten percent of every hour, even when we stay on point, on mission, and have developed a mission statement that is actually clear and not caloric. In other words, we not only have missions, we have inboxes. We have actions we intend to take and connections we intend to keep. We have things we have to do before we do what we want to do – even though Stephen Covey insists that the best way to live is to do what you want to do first.

Developing a mission statement is mostly a matter of putting our hopes on a diet and putting them into a humble, manageable form. You can't create a new way of doing commerce or redistribute money to working people or even create heaven on earth. But you *can* do your part of each of those. A mission statement says which portion you will love onto your plate.

Writing the new Etsy.org mission statement involved all these boilerplate mission statement challenges. It also had a little magic to it. Maybe it was Matt Stinchcomb's father's thesaurus, which made its way into our conference room. It was so much better that the online ones we were using. Maybe it was the ease with which three people who didn't really know each other very well traded words and ideas and misgivings and "aha" moments. Mostly it was the fun around the verbs.

"Evoke" got everybody going. We loved it and were provoked by it. Evoke made the tilt towards the more spiritual in the entrepreneurial. It held a bold hope that human beings have what it takes to create new commerce and that "all" we have to do is tend it and evoke it. It also tilted us towards emerging human capacity and against Etsy being "just" another training institution for entrepreneurs who want to make money. (Nothing wrong with money as long as it regenerates.)

We knew we had three non-negotiables in the mission statement. One was that the person was as transformed as the product. By regenerative businesses we meant regenerating the business *maker and* the business – both, not either-or. The second was that we wanted to recognize wisdom as well as skill. We wanted *doing* and *being* to shake hands. The third was that Etsy.com would be almost as happy with it as we were.

There was also a fourth thing we wanted, which was to acknowledge regeneration businesses as places based and relying on good old evolutionary theory. The business adapts to the environment and then the environment adapts to the business, and then the cycle repeats. The person involved morphs just as much – responding, adapting, and changing, right down to the bones or the genes. We wanted to name ecological interdependence as a kind of pedagogy, or way of learning. This "fourth" just didn't fit until we realized that building regenerative businesses is fundamentally ecological and evolutionary. Saying the word "regeneration" implies evolution, place, adaptation, and ongoing cycles of learning. The learning doesn't stop. It cycles.

With the word regeneration, we meant a unique pedagogy or way of teaching and learning, one that will invite people to redefine the meaning of success and that will take them to the places that scare or depress them. Regeneration gives permission to despair and harnesses the energy of despair. Much commerce has come to an ecological, environmental, and economic dead end. Wisdom starts there.

Wisdom

When it comes to taming the time famine, or creating a new self or a new business, we don't need more knowledge, we need more wisdom. Wisdom involves *unlearning* as well as learning. Learning and unlearning are partners, not enemies. Learning apprentices itself to wisdom about who we are in a particular place and about what that place *is*. Again, it's a matter of both, not either-or. Learning will do and doing will learn. Capacity will be evoked and regenerated. These are the big ideas that will form Etsy's small practice of regenerating businesses, one by one, person by person, and they can work for you, too. That other spacious verb, "foster," will show up in community as well.

The grace part

What I am trying to show here about mission coherence is that it is an *aim*, not an *achievement*, a well-thought-through script created by mature adults using executive function. It needs constant self-criticism. It is rarely achieved. A little humour in it goes a long way. By grace, you aim. By grace, you do not always achieve. But the more grace present in your aim, the more likely you will achieve.

The apostle Paul is important here. We don't become coherent by grace as a way to achieve more, or to beat the time famine at its own instrumental game. Grace as a script is not a strategy. It lives beyond the utilitarianism of time management techniques. Grace scripts you for strength and capacity, for sure. But it is not experienced as a *way* or a *method* to get strength and capacity. Paul spoke often of grace as the forgiveness of our sins, as in when we don't achieve what we wanted to achieve. He asks the playful question, "What then, shall we sin more, so that grace may abound?" If we failed more, wouldn't we achieve more grace? Nope. Just the opposite. Grace is the freedom to experiment enough to fail a lot, and to try again in the morning.

Conclusion

When you get to the task and settle down to it in a favourite room with a good brew of your favourite coffee or tea or beer, note that you are in the place where you will cohere your own personal mission. When you get started, get excited. You are about to get a positive form of graceful control of your own life and its aims. You are about to have fun. You are about to get really involved in your own evolution as a person, and as a creature, and as a part of the normal human race.

You may have lost your sense of wonder, or your curiosity about yourself and your genomic place in the larger matters called life and world, but you are about to find it again. Go slow. Go simple. Go humble. Go now.

Questions for reflection and discussion

The best pattern for writing a mission statement is the simplest one. Just answer these questions, without a lot of fuss and bother. What's up? So what? What's next? Turn the process into a conversation with yourself.

1. If someone says to you, "just suck it up," can you respond, "I would but my vacuum cleaner bag is full." How often do you just suck it up, instead of refusing to suck it up?
2. Meditate on – and if you are with a group discuss – this statement by Walter Brueggemann: "Resurrection faith is not something only for funerals. It is a question of the kind of world that can be spoken by poets in the face of a world that has failed. The alternative to such a dangerous faith is to join in the cover-up. That of course never yields vitality."
3. Can you recall a time when you accidentally stepped into mission coherence? When you knew you had to *say* something or *do* something because otherwise the *you* that is *you* would be too violated? Why did that happen? Share your story.

4. When have you experienced regeneration?
5. If you already have a mission statement, would you like to revise it? If so, why? If not, why not?

Prayer

O God, make our days so full of what we choose to do that we feast on time. Amen.

Focus for the week

Find out from people you respect what kind of coring, cohering mission statement they have for their life? How did they get it? How do they change it, if they *do* change it? What is their process for evaluation? Are these people who live in famine or feast? Assess them quietly.

CHAPTER FIVE

When Feast Becomes Fun

One of the main ways you can assess your time diet – and whether it is more feast than famine – is to remember the last time you did something you didn't have to do. Beyond the strategies we have been suggesting – facing our mortality, non-participation and resistance to your marching orders to stay busy, having a mission statement for the life you want – there are many smaller and less weighty indicators for and ways to move towards feast.

We are in famine when all of our time is taken up doing what we *have* to do. We are in feast when we do both what we *have* to do *and* spend some time doing what we *don't have to do*. I call the latter "goofballing," and like to be known as an expert goofballer. I don't put this skill on my resumé, but fun *is* central to my mission statement. Some activity may be spiritual nurture for public capacity, but it is only part of my mission statement if I am having fun doing it. An opportunity may arise for me to provide a less punitive spiritual narrative as a serious challenge to the political and economic status quo, but if I am not having fun trying to do that, it is not my mission. You can see why immediately. Why would I punish myself as a way to challenge the ways our systems punishment people?

Most of us have equally troubling conflicts within our own aims and our own aimlessness. Something "fits" on one level, we may feel passionate about or drawn to something, but does following that passion or interest *always* fits with the "big picture" of our mission statement? Not necessarily. Despite what I said previously, maybe we *do* sin so that grace may abound. We do miss our mark so that we can articulate our mark more clearly. Or maybe we don't do it on purpose, but we can certainly learn from our near-misses. We can refine the mark.

Either way, goofballing is one way to minimize those conflicts. Below I will offer some examples of how *I* goofball in the hope that they will give you permission to join fun, pleasure, and the "great unnecessary" to your life and its mission. But first, I want to show how energy exchanges when we are having fun, how waste itself is important. Wasting time is important to enjoying time, which is what it means to feast in time.

Energy exchanges in feast

While sitting around waiting for that time when all waste will become energy, I was delighted to discover that the Galapagos Islands are going to get there in 2017. All waste becoming energy? Yes. The Galapagos plan will use all the waste it produces to create all the energy it needs. They will be even with themselves. Whatever additional energy they need they will produce. They are close already and will fully arrive at their destination on time.

That is what we know as ecological sense. It is also spiritual sense. We get even with ourselves. Ideally, we rest the right amount, work the right amount, and don't get bored by rest. We get energized for work by play and rest. That is the kind of energy equilibrium for which we aim.

But permit me to muse on whether we can be really equal with ourselves. Let me define that balance a little more carefully. Will what we *put in* be the equivalent of what we *put out*? Will moral energy coalesced become moral power released into the universe? Will there be any waste? Or will all the input go straight to output? In other words, even when we wisely use waste and the unnecessary activity of leisure, will there still be waste that cannot be fruitfully used?

If you have ever done any community work, you will feel these questions sharply. You will know there *has* to be some waste, some lack of human kindness, some stupidity involved. My office just lost a passel of receipts and now I can't get paid for a long trip I took. Now we are all "wasting" energy finding them or reproducing them.

You already know the statement, "let it ride, he is just another bozo on the bus," or some similarly cynical self-protection. You probably had other things to do today or this season, but once you felt a positive buzz, you joined the hive. That "joining something positive" probably meant that you or your office lost some receipts – something else *didn't* happen because of what *did* happen. But such moments don't have to constitute waste. They may instead be learning opportunities. Most of us learn from our failures more than we learn from our successes.

There is also waste involved with lost vacations. Then again, who can vacation at times like these? When the wave of work energy comes, we ride it. When people organize and activate themselves, there is a renewable energy that is stronger than solar or wind energy. It multiples. It's catching. You want to be there. You are being refreshed and revived in the same ways that vacationing or self-emptying or Sabbath-keeping makes possible.

What is more problematic as potential waste is not actually measurable in individual terms. It will only be known in the "after." How can we know that we are making a decision for feast, amidst famine, if we follow a positive, life-giving endeavour? What will happen to what we omit from our lives? How do we make decisions, or find the strength to make decisions, that commit us anew in such a way that we are able to break old, harmful promises? Much time famine comes from this quandary.

Learning how to say no means learning how to say yes. Here I want you to commit to renewable things, not to the dead end things that wear you down. Goofballing – or following a positive vibe – is almost always the right decision. If you have to omit something else, tell people what you are doing and why you are doing it. Go for the joy and be *known* for the person who goes for the joy. You will be so renewed that you will find a way to keep up with your less life-giving obligations. Energy creates energy. Waste also creates energy, especially if we balance ourselves correctly.

Often, we pray for big changes in our world. To employ some biblical metaphors, we pray that the mountains and hills will burst into song. That the trees of the fields will clap their hands. Surely the mountains will be brought low and the valleys will rise up. *None* of this will happen if we just keep obligations going. *All* of this will happen if we have fun while being obligated. We *do* have obligations and we should and can meet them. But if they exhaust us, perpetually and perennially, we need to change our obligations. Our primary obligation is to our own energy and its sustainability.

In time feast, power changes its meaning and transcends the electrical. *Real* power is the power to make a positive impact. Real power is the capacity to disrupt. Real power is the capacity to laugh. There is a crucible and a crucialness to being a power. You know you are a power by whether or not other people take you seriously. You know you are a power by what other people get away with saying about you, or to you. Whether other people want to copy you or emigrate to you. Or by click testing: did they read or share? Power shows up in buzz. Power shows up in positive energy. You will have more positive energy the more you have fun, especially while fulfilling your obligations.

Think like the Galapagos. Think and pray that all this energy we are putting into doing what we *have* to do is spent to give us a chance to what we *want* to do. And watch out, always, for that word "do." You are not a human doing. You are a human being. You don't need to worry so much about what you are doing or "not getting done." Hear the sneaky fear of mortality in that statement. Rather, you need to worry about your *being* – and goofballing is the best way to worry about your being. You need to worry less about your doing, unless you want to become or remain a human doing, not a human being.

Stop worrying about worrying

Worry is the uninvited invasion of the present by the past or the future. The past invades by regrets. What if I just hadn't said that or done that, or what if she hadn't said that to me, or he hadn't done that to me? If those bad things hadn't happened, then I could be happy now. Since they did, I can't. We go over the past like a dog gnaws a bone. There is no meat there, but that doesn't keep us from chewing.

The future's army crosses our borders with less definition. What if I lose my job? What if I can't lose this weight? What if her tests come out badly? What if the Lyme disease doesn't respond to medication?

Both the past and the future can invade the country of the present, occupy and colonize it, and refuse to let it go out by day or by night. Especially at night, worries like to have their way with us. Those that don't invade our conscious life show up in our unconscious and nag.

The most acute kind of worry is when we get down on ourselves for worrying. We not only worry, we worry about how much we worry. "I know I shouldn't worry, but I do." We jump into the well of worry and spiral down. But still, it is possible to climb out of the well one rung on the ladder at a time. It is possible to *own* your own land, to live on the corner of "here and now" and to free yourself from foreign occupation. Think of this process as a Boston Tea Party, a revolution by the forces of the present, in the present, overthrowing the wicked spirits with the good ones. The aim is to get off the saucer and into the teacup of life.

Spirit is the power

If willpower could prevent worry from "warting" you, it would already have worked. If playing *Don't Worry, Be Happy* over and over every day could keep worry from wasting you, you'd be living in the here and now already. If the famous poster "What, me worry?" could humour you into worry-free living, you'd not be reading this far.

The rungs on the ladder out of the well of worry are spiritual. They don't fix the worries so much as enable us to climb above them. The great sociologist Robert Bellah said that religion is the imagination of another reality. When we learn to let worry go, we do so because we want another reality to come in. We want to live in what Canadian theologian Douglas John Hall calls the good news, which he defines as "the permission and the commandment to enter difficulty with hope." Permission. Commandment. Enter. Difficulty. With hope. That is the spiritual power that comes from a dimension deeper and wider than the deviltry of difficulty. Spiritual power is *above* and *within* and *deeper*. It occupies another level in the *now*. Spiritual power is the power to say yes to fun in our aim in life.

Things said or done have injured many people. Abuse, large and small, is real. So is injury. Many people have good reason to worry about the continuation of their job or good health. Fear, large and small, is real. When we borrow the power of the spirit to live in the present, we do so trusting that its power is larger than the big stuff we worry about. We imagine ourselves as agents and actors in our lives, as opposed to victims. We become the subjects not the objects of our own sentences. We may not be able to control the Lyme disease, but we can control our attitude towards it.

"We can?" you say. Wondering if Pollyanna is speaking?

Yes, we can. The power of Spirit is larger than the power of any injury.

The power of the practical

Perhaps you need more hope than you have. Perhaps you only hear the murmur of an invitation to enter your trouble with hope. Perhaps you are way down deep in the well, below the ladder and need help to even get to the first rung.

Permit me to give you the practical reasons not to worry. It doesn't help. It wastes time. It blocks positive energy. It goes quickly to sounding off, which is the opposite of the high art of complaining. In a complaint, we hope and intend a positive outcome. In whining and sounding off, we are just hearing ourselves talk. Worry that leads to complaint can be justified; worry that expresses despair leads to more despair and is impractical. Even if you can't get to the first rung on the ladder, right now, you sure don't want to go down deeper. Plus, nobody ever climbed a mountain thinking they couldn't do it.

Like most people, I have plenty of excuses for worrying. I can't remember my passwords. I was on hold with a bank that charged me $59 for an annual fee on a card I don't have. My offspring may have to live through a changed climate, after all that money I spent on braces. My hollyhocks have a disease. These are perfectly good reasons to worry, and I hope you will join me in legitimating them.

Worrying, however, will do nothing about a single one of these things. As the old song says, "Worry gets us nowhere, absolutely nowhere, worry gets us nowhere at all."

Some of us work in business where the word "results" rings in our ears all day long. If you look at the track record of worry, you discover something very quickly. It brings only negative results. Firing worry from your team will bring results in peace, power, and energy. Keeping worry on your team will do the opposite.

When we stop worrying about worrying

What does it look like to be worry free? We symbolically toss all of the enemy's tea into the spiritual sea. We don't cooperate with our persecutor. We take one rung on the ladder at a time, as our energy permits. We don't give ourselves more to do in any given moment than we can do. We do piecework and we do it well. I clean my whole house this way, one corner a day.

Most of all, we are living in the present. The past and the future are no longer our masters.

If you agree with the wasted waste of worrying – not the kind the Galapagos recommends – then consider this. Put yourself on a worry budget. You can worry five times a day. Then you have to do something else. I tried this method last winter, which was full of snowstorms and cold. I could only complain about the weather five times a day. I had lots of fun telling people I was over-budget. We had some good laughs and that made us all warmer.

What follows will be some idiosyncratic ways of goofballing. You may imitate. You may also choose not to imitate. The best part of goofballing is how custom-designed it has to be.

Goofballing: Example One

I have kept a record of every full moon I have seen for the last two decades. A friend gave me a book called *Walk When the Moon Is Full*. The gift gave me permission to watch for the moon like a hawk and to write down my location as I saw it. Just remembering the location helped me remember my mood and my sense of who I was then.

The point is, I don't *have* to walk while the moon is full. I *like* to walk while the moon is full. I do miss a moon every now and then. But rarely. My book is almost full of annotations. I show the book to my family and friends every now and then, just to amuse them.

Goofballing: Example Two

I have a chiminea, one of those small pudgy Mexican fireplaces. I got it at a yard sale for ten dollars. It could be my favourite possession. In the mornings, I gather sticks for it. Sometimes I gather sticks in the city to bring to the country. Often in the winter I don't get to the country for weeks at a time. I get a lot of sticks ready. Gathering these sticks is necessary to the pleasure of a night fire. But I don't really *have* to have a night fire. I could omit that pleasure from my life, especially if I didn't have any sticks around. The stick gathering is a kind of walking meditation. I don't really have to do it at all.

Goofballing: Example Three

Most artists are goofballing. They don't really have to do what they are doing. But they do it.

On the Hudson River, Melissa McGill's installation *Constellation* drags the stars to earth just about any night off the Beacon shore or from the train between Cold Spring and Beacon, New York. This magic was created by a woman who lived in Beacon long enough to know that there was an island close by that was not being put to use. Not that islands need to be put to use, of course. But if you install LED lights on top of long poles on an island, the stars in the sky can talk to the stars in our imagination all night long. Her installation is utterly magical, as the LED lights go on as dusk falls and the real stars start their gradual blinking. When she asked the contractor to help her put in this utterly unnecessary impracticality, he said no. It was just too expensive to bring the poles over that would be strong enough to be dug deep enough to hold the lights. They'd just blow down if they were skinny.

Then the contractor realized. "You're going to do this, right?" The feast part and the feisty part of goofballing was right there. Of course, it was expensive. It was also unnecessary. Melissa was going to do this and she did. She might even argue that the nonessential was absolutely essential.

Goofballing: Example Four

I build rubber band balls. I do so somewhat compulsively. I love it when I find a red rubber band as it adds colour to the balls. Once I had to take three kids to a congressman's office. Congressman Rangel was his name. He went off during our appointment to keep the children's father from being deported. We were left alone in his office for over an hour. We made rubber band balls. It was a distraction, a way to keep the children from being totally terrified. When the congressman came back and told us that the deportation was off, we gave him our rubber band ball. Now, whenever I see the nine-year-old boy who was most entranced with the making of the ball and its twining and twining, he asks me if I have made any new balls. I always say yes, because I have. He is 15 now and much too old to be talking about rubber band balls. But his father is still here.

Goofballing: Example Five

I like to define goofballing as the art of noticing what you have already seen. Once, I saw the deep blue wine berries of fall differently than I had seen them before. I have seen a million fall wine berries, but these grabbed my attention in an important way.

Often considered a weed, wine berries are blousy and fat, dominating and unplanted. They look like those shelves in antique stores, where blue glasses and vases and pitchers cling together for colour. They have a way of getting whatever nourishment they need wherever they are. More leaf than berry, you have to sleuth the blues. They self-plant and self-seed, the way Vandana Shiva says Indian women did before Monsanto tried to criminalize their sustainable skills. Once there is a wine berry in a spot, they won't go away. They will always come back. No winter frightens them.

The same weekend I had seen the wine berries anew – and learned to admire their annual tenacity – I saw fall watercress in the market. I hadn't seen watercress for years, not since one Pennsylvania dawn when the green challenged the white snow on the ground. I realized that I know joy in the morning and the watercress, the weeds and the blues. When I give myself the time to notice what I have already seen, I often get to the refreshment stand, where I can drink gladness without paying for it. I call noticing a low-cost form of personal entertainment.

The green of watercress and the blue of wine berries may be all I need to remember. That, plus my time and place, my here and now, my then and again. It is so much fun to wake up the next day after you have noticed something you thought you had already seen, and be happy that you knew how to notice.

Goofballing: Example Six

I may be 68, but I am an early feminist. I may be an aging hippie, but I prefer the title senior hippie. I was well advised to tell my grandchildren to call me Bubbe instead of Grandma. "Grandma" would make me feel old; "Bubbe" would amuse me. You get my drift, coded in apologies for having gotten old while I wasn't looking. I still want to be the next Verlyn Klinkenborg. I want his perch as a country writer to whom city people listen. Or to be the chaplain at Google and let them know how much pastors know about privacy and confidentiality. I want to retire without becoming retiring, age alert to blues and greens. I want to know this season as well as a fall wine berry does. I want to emerge from the cold with the courage of the water's cress. I want to be able to remember without distortion and to save seeds, knowing one time and place is always yielding to the next.

When we play with age, we are also playing with time. I often quip that I am looking forward to being a burden on my family. Most people laugh wryly. I actually don't mean it so much as hope that I will know how to be 68 when I am 68, 69 when I am 69, feeble when I am feeble, etc. I hate it when people say, "You don't look your age." Why would I not want to look my age? Why would I want to be somebody else's age?

The art of play or what I am calling goofballing here often has to do with reversing the field. Whatever everybody else is saying, say something different. It can be fun.

Questions for reflection and discussion

1. When was the last time you did something you didn't have to do? How often do you do things you don't have to do? Are you a list maker? Do you ever go off your list?
2. Who are some people you admire for the way they enjoy life? What is their secret? Can you borrow from them?
3. Do you think it is frivolous to goofball? Why? Do you think it is wrong to be silly? Why? How would you describe your own sense of humour?
4. What percentage of your mental time and space is given over to worry? What kind of a worrier are you? Can you imagine a whole day without worrying? What is the worst thing that could happen?
5. When you think of the word waste, as in "waste of time," what does that concept tell you? Do you think there is anything that is really a waste? How have things that felt like waste transformed themselves for you, or in you?

Prayer

Release me from the power of obligation, O God, so that I may freely choose my obligations, have the energy I need to fulfill them, and the wisdom to know how to have fun while being a *doing* human being, who is also a *being* human doing, just as you created me. Amen.

Focus for the week

Begin to turn your waste into energy. Begin to waste time intentionally so as to learn to value it beyond its production capacities. Learn what renews you and do lots of renewing. Give yourself permission to be renewed.

CHAPTER SIX

Down-and-Dirty How To
FROM FAMINE TO FEAST IN 52 WEEKS

So far in this work we have talked about the systemic sources of the time famine and how they show up in our work and in our family and in our soul. We have offered some solutions. One of them is writing a personal mission statement that encapsulates your personal coherence. Another is about joining spiritual to digital technologies. These are ways to approach the "how" after we know the "why" about our aim for feast. We have talked about the importance of not worrying, and about the importance of goofballing, although we certainly don't want to overdo the importance of that. You can't make a *task* out of goofballing! In each of these directions and directives, we aim for feast instead of settling for famine. Aim is the important word; we aim to master as much of our life as we can, rather than to let it master us. We don't want to be victims. We know we can't be victors. But we aim for more victory than victimhood.

Limits

Now, it is important to be clear about four things.

What you *can't* do. The circumstances of your life may keep you somewhat bound, either to work or family.

What you *can* do about what you *can't* do. You can make friends with what you can't do, embrace your circumstances, and refuse to whine about them.

What you *can* do. Minimally, you can find a small corner of freedom in which you do nothing you *have* to do. I call this goofballing. You may have another name for your uselessness. Maximally, you can find a whole room or whole house in which to enjoy recreation.

What you *can't* do about what you *can* do. Don't brag if you achieve freedom and feast. Help others to find it by being humble about it. And surely, don't take credit for it. Understand that you have received the gift of freedom from God, or from a power higher than you are. Be grateful while being humble.

Sabbath revisited

I know we discussed the importance of Sabbath-keeping in the first chapter, before we go into the down-and-dirty renewable, and more importantly, *renewing* guide, I want to visit Sabbath once again. In other words, I want to draw an explicit connection between Sabbath-keeping and the "practice" suggestions that follow.

Here's the thing. It is important to check our century pride at the door. People have been keeping a good Sabbath for a long time, way before we had the kind of time famine that we have now. Sabbath is a time-honoured way to feast and, if we want to feast, we need to discover some new ways of keeping the Sabbath, while understanding the value and virtue of the "old" ways, which developed out of a different cultural and economic need. Ideally, we'll understand these weekly practices that I'm about to suggest, these new ways to keep Sabbath, as being part of an ancient, universal, and doable lineage.

But first, here are a few suggestions to consider specifically related to Sabbath, or to the concept of Sabbath. Because of the centrality of these concepts, I want to hold them separate from the 52 suggestions for weekly practice, which follow.

1. Tell yourself that you *may* keep Sabbath, not that you *must*.

2. If you can keep a full day on Saturday or Sunday for nothing but worship and quiet, please do. But if you can't keep Sabbath the way your ancestors did, figure out something new.
3. Keep a 21st-century Sabbath – you don't have to have a biblical Sabbath, or follow the same traditions (or lack of them) that your family did.
4. Custom-design your Sabbath practice to fit your job, your family, and your commute. Experiment with a Friday night pattern, or a Monday morning pattern. Keep trying until you can develop something that has a soothing regularity.

Renewable, sustainable, repeatable

Here are my suggestions for a renewable and renewing ritual that will take you to feast week by week. You don't have to try all of the suggestions I make here, but you *should* try some of them. Not all of these will apply to you. Some of you will already be so able to feast, from time to time, that you will want to help others do the same. Others will be so starving that you will find even these simple suggestions daunting. If you reject one week's direction, make up your own. Custom-design your weekly practice. You can do it.

Just like the mission coherence, these practices are not for experts only. They are for ordinary people dealing with the ordinary stressors of ordinary life. Thus, the spiritual technologies I suggest here are adaptable and are made to be custom-designed for your place in your world. They give permission for you to design your own coherence and your own way to it.

Let me repeat: you really don't want to be a victim. You want to be the master and driver of your life. But because the time famine is so serious a matter, and the powers set against human feasting on time are so strong, it's not likely you will fully achieve freedom from victimization, even if you do everything here. But you will not consent to it either. Non-participation in the systems that hurt you is very important, even if the systems still keep a bit of noose around your neck.

You are going to aim, instead, to use spiritual practices that *aim* you towards feast. In this week-by-week summary, you will find a way to be constantly moving beyond victim status. You will find coherence. And you will be so much less afraid of death and dying than you ever have been. You will not fear premature death or actual death. You will know you are living, because you are aiming for feast. You will have accepted God's creation of you, and God's promise to *keep* re-creating you. Re-creation is recreation. You will achieve the maximum freedom from the time famine the more you play (and not work) at achieving it.

Finally, try to take the whole week to do each of these suggestions. You have time. You actually don't have time *not* to go slowly on changing your spiritual habits. And yes, you'll get to repeat this every year if you want to.

52 Weeks

1. Take your time. Take. Your. Time. Do everything at half speed for an hour or so each day.

2. Ritualize your life. Do email at set times in the morning or afternoon – or when you decide – and live free of it the rest of the day. Tell people what you are doing. "You can expect an answer after 4:30."

3. Ritualize your weekly exercise program. Let your body and soul say hello to each other in a morning or evening walk; yoga on Mondays, Wednesdays, and Fridays; stretching or weight lifting on Tuesdays and Thursdays. Make a plan for you. Write it down. Do it. Do it as a Sabbath.

4. Find a place with water – a river, a lake, a mountain spring – or put a bowl of fresh water on your desk. Touch the water on a regular basis, either once an hour or once a day or once a week.

5. Always eat lunch or always eat dinner. Eat a real sit-down meal on some regular basis, perhaps with a tablecloth or cloth napkin you keep in your desk drawer. People who eat without ritual or grace at table get into a lot of trouble. It is not

accidental that Sabbath-keeping is so connected with food. Changing the way we eat is one of the most serious means by which capitalism makes its way with us. If you really "don't have time to eat," always put a tablecloth on your desk. It will be a signal to the masters that they are not in charge. If you find yourself eating "out," or "on the go," or out of Styrofoam or plastic or paper bags, buy yourself a good carry bowl. Eat from a beautiful bowl.

6. How is your aim? Are you hitting any of your marks? Give yourself a ruthless evaluation. Share it with someone you trust.

7. Figure out when the next full moon is. Enjoy it. Mark down the dates of the full moons on your calendar and integrate them into your Sabbath.

8. Call up an old friend and ask how he or she is. Don't request anything from them. Just enjoy them.

9. Write your funeral service. Every couple of Sabbaths, rewrite it. Review your will. Embrace your mortality.

10. If you used to play a sport as a kid, go watch some kids play that sport. Remember what you liked about it.

11. Do something you have never done before, like go to a matinee or read some cartoons.

12. Resolve a problem that you have worried to death. Either resolve it or put it in a box marked "string too short to be saved," or something absurd like that. Resolve to open it up every fourth Sabbath to see how it is doing.

13. If you have a pet, give yourself a special treat and enjoy the pet on a special Sabbath.

14. Take a long nap some afternoon.

15. Clean out all your closets and get rid of a certain percentage of what you have. Declutter with spiritual gusto.

16. Redecorate your entire house, doing one small space at a time.

17. Ask yourself what you are looking forward to. Ask your best friend or partner the same question. Take one strong step towards it, even if it means booking tickets or completing a project.

18. Write a holiday or seasonal letter and edit it every couple of weeks. Send it out at Christmas as your best work ever. Make it funny. Let it sparkle. Make it glitter. Make believe you are a great writer living a great life and that you want everybody to know about it.

19. Turn hard tasks into a joy. Whatever hard task you have to do today, the one you call beyond our "pay level," imagine it as a joy, a privilege, an occasion for ecstasy. Stand in awe at how hard your day is. Give thanks for the difficulty. Divide it into tasks. Don't try to do everything at once.

20. My mother called her friend every day at 10:30 in the morning. As a girl, I listened to their joyous connection, even though they were mostly complaining about their husbands. I email one of my friends.

21. Go slow, go simple. Just take the next step. Don't worry about all the steps.

22. Who criticizes you? Who gets to criticize you? Ask them to go home. Put them in the box next to your biggest worry. Let them enjoy each other on their shelf.

23. Is there anything wrong with hard work or being tired? I think not. I think rather the opposite. Spend the week figuring out why you are tired? On behalf of what? To whom do you give permission to make you tired?

24. What are your spiritual practices? A spiritual practice is a deepening of the *always* and the *everyday*. It is washing the dishes as though you like to do it, or flossing your teeth as though you love your teeth, rather than just as a way to keep the dentist from guilt-tripping you. A spiritual practice is also pretty much anything that tussles with the pragmatic and takes pragmatism into something deeper than its obvious and worthy utility. Practice is not the opposite of pragmatic so much as its underwear, what you wear close to your skin. I pick up twigs in the morning for nighttime fires. It helps me have a mini-Sabbath.

25. Everyone sees the writing on the wall. Most of us assume it is addressed to someone else. Everyone knows that we should be grateful for the food on our plates, and the teeth in our mouths. Very few of us experience gratitude. Spiritual practices train and trick and prod our unconscious into consciousness. The word "Duh" comes to mind. Practice saying "thank you" – often.

26. I love my Cuban friend who says that we use too much toothpaste in the U.S. He is making a spiritual comment about a material matter. What constitutes too much? Or too little? For you? Today? This week?

27. Inner realities manage outward difficulties. Do you believe it? Pay attention to your week and then ask yourself the same question: "Do you believe it?"

28. Get or make a *mezuzah*, a Jewish religious object placed on the door to your home. Touch it on the way out and on your way in. Regard your goings out and your comings in.

29. I wonder how many women have accomplished as much as I have and still feel as unworthy as I do? Who is telling you that you are unworthy of enjoying your time? There was supposed to be a time after proving yourself. When was that? When will that be, for you? My friend says she is "a barnacle

looking for a boat." She is unhappily retired. She has too much time. She had wanted to score a ten on the dismount. She feels idle and useless. In other words, Sabbath is also about getting outside of yourself. Think about my friend and how she connects to you.

30. What would it mean for you to become a spiritual entrepreneur? Could you get rich that way? Design your business. Meet Herman of the film *Herman's House*. He was in solitary confinement for almost four decades. He designed a house for himself, with the help of a friend on the outside. He lived in his imagination. Imagine yourself as a spiritual entrepreneur.

31. How much does it matter that we "give back" or "give forward" or give to others? What are your obligations to others? Why, how, and when do you give?

32. Experts tell us that authority involves controlling yourself, not others. Authority is self-control, not getting the pack to fall in line with you, or you to fall in line with the pack. I like Jesus because he had that kind of authority. He wasn't willing to take orders from a tired religious establishment, nor was he willing to give orders. Instead, he made a large refusal to have an enemy or to be an enemy. It was a powerful form of love. What authority do you have over your own time?

33. Do something this week you have never done before. Like riding the Q train out to Coney Island to listen to live poetry in the last car at 8 p.m. on Saturday nights. I was always so jealous of the people who could do that and then I did it and feasted time and poetry and the Q train.

34. Spend time this week thinking about who you will be in early dotage, mid dotage, late dotage. Enjoy him or her in your fantasy of time. Are you going to embrace aging, or fear it?

35. Time management is important. It is a skill. It is a science. We should all take a course in it. And then we should learn how to pitch high and inside, or low and outside. We should choose a specialty. Or have half the activity and double our impact. Or think fewer, finer. In other words, what is the one thing you should be doing? Get rid of the rest.

36. Give 100 blessings a day, then be off duty.

37. Find an ancient practice, like knitting or davening or the rosary, and use it to still your body.

38. Take your heart to the downtrodden. Understand the words trodden down. Remove your boot. Caring about those who are oppressed all around will make you see time in a completely different way than as self-control or as *incurvatus in se*, as curving in on oneself. Co-sign a loan for someone, if you have money.

39. Tame your technology. Don't become the tool of your tools. If you have already become the tool of your tool, unbecome one. Anticipate days not minutes to accomplish this patterned liberation.

40. Become a proud imperfectionist. Fail regularly at turning the time famine into a time feast. And then try again.

41. When you run hard and long, are you just trying to catch up with yourself? Or is there another reason? Are you being chased, or trying to outrun something? Can you stop long enough to catch up with yourself? "When things settle down." Spend the week thinking about what that would mean to you. What would that look like in terms of how you live?

42. Where will you be in five years? How will you get there? We know we are feasting in time when we can take long glances at a long and good life. Not worried glances, but happy ones.

43. Imagine disasters and be ready for their profound interruptions. Rebecca Solnit, who wrote *Wanderlust: A History of Walking*, has also written *A Paradise Built in Hell: The Extraordinary Communities that Arise in Disaster*. Isn't the time famine an everyday disaster? Solnit says that we fall *together*, as opposed to falling apart, during disasters like the San Francisco Earthquake, or 9–11, or Katrina, or Sandy. We find the "power from below." We learn that our neighbour is our greatest asset, not our greatest enemy. How can power from below, and falling together, and understanding each other as assets help us with the time famine? Indulge "retrospective basking" and love to tell our story. How can you bask in the moment as well as in the histories you share with others? Visit a neighbour. Or hold a potluck for the neighbourhood. See who comes. Send a note to those who don't.

44. An ordinary day. Spend the week thinking about how your ordinary days will be different if you become a person of the time feast. Think of this 52-week outline as a diet to which you commit yourself and that will help you become spiritually and religiously "lighter." What will you look like and be like on an ordinary day?

45. Eroticize your Sabbath. Jews think it a *Mitzvah* or blessing to make love on the Sabbath. If this suggestion makes you wonder when the last time was you made love, pray that through with those whom you love.

46. An ordinary afternoon. Are you a person who needs a siesta or a power nap or both? Do you take one? If not, why not? Make napping part of your spiritual practice, beginning now.

47. Do everything you can to go to sleep at a "regular" time. Keep technology from the last thing you do at night or the first thing you do in the morning. Pray instead for those you love, when you rise and when you bed down.

48. What happens when your pattern changes? How do you accommodate change? Is travel a game-changer for you? Positively or negatively? How do you stay normal on the road? How often do you need to break your pattern? Who breaks it and why? Is it a feast to break habits or a new kind of tricky famine?

49. An ordinary holiday, Christmas, or Hanukkah, or Eid al-Fitr. Put an annual sacred observance into your ordinary day or ordinary week. Plan for ritual. Many families like mine take a big hike after the Thanksgiving turkey. Plan on not going into time famine during "holidays."

50. Send a letter of resignation to the time famine.

51. Review these suggestions for practicing time feast and analyze which ones you rejected and which ones you accepted. Why one and not the other?

52. A rite of passage: Congratulate yourself on becoming a person of feast. Give thanks for having a great year. And start over, and over, and over again.

Questions for reflection and discussion

1. If not now, when? Why not now? What's wrong with now? What's right with now?
2. How good a procrastinator are you? Why do you procrastinate? Who knows that you procrastinate?
3. If you were to write your spiritual life resumé, what accomplishments would you list on it? How would you describe your desired life position?
4. Find someone with whom to share your notebook. Ask if they want to join you in a year of aiming for feast.

Prayer (Haiku)

Hard, hard, hard, hard Task
Soften into strength as joy
Task untied, tongue freed.
Time Tamed.

Focus for the week

Get a good notebook and design your down-and-dirty year. Make believe this is the biggest project of your life and that you are being paid $100,000 to do it. You want the plan to be superb. God is your benefactor. You are the beneficiary. Measure your progress.

CONCLUSION

Guidelines for Small Groups

You may want to read and use this book by yourself. You may find it just right for evoking your ability to "feast in time." On the other hand, you may want a companion or two, or three or more, along the way. You may already be part of a book club or a Bible-study group or a coffee klatch and want to move from time famine to time feast with these friends at your side. If you want to bring a small group together during Lent or at any other time during the year, think of what follows as options. Think of them as guidelines, not rules. Think of them as trail markers, like the white blaze on the tree in the wood that keeps you on the path.

1. Set a time and place. There are six chapters in the book so it makes sense to plan for six group sessions. Since we're aiming for time feast, make the time easy – like breakfast Mondays, or lunch Tuesdays, or dinner Thursdays. Before or after church on Sundays can be an easy time if you want the group to be open and include those who can only come once or twice. An open group makes for less intimacy, but has the advantage of greater diversity and attendance possibilities.
2. If people have children, figure out how to rotate childcare, or pay for it. If people need transportation, figure out how to travel together or car pool. If you need food, rotate responsi-

bility for bringing and making it – and for cleaning up. Be sure there is a leader each time you meet. Make sure she or he knows how to lead. Rotating leadership gives everybody a turn and everybody some practice at leading. If your pastor wants to lead, surely let him or her do that. In other words, make sure someone is in charge of making sure the airtime gets shared, and make sure that person has permission to lead. Rotate hosts for each event so that somebody is first to arrive and greet, and last to leave and lock up. Make the appropriate spiritual technology also very practical. When details get in the way of the program, watch out. But without attention to details, the space won't clear for the spiritually renewing experience.

3. The suggested questions for reflection and discussion included at the end of each chapter are exactly that – suggestions, which can be adapted, changed, or ignored entirely. They can be used privately or as fodder for group discussion.
4. Remember that in every group setting, people should have the freedom to speak, and just as important, *not* to speak in any given moment, or in response to any given question or topic.
5. Make sure the conversation "space" is safe for disagreement and exchanges that might be emotion-filled. Don't expect every session to satisfy every person. Acknowledge that renewal and refreshment may involve some personal engagement and possibly even some group conflict – not the mean kind, but the kind that forces us to the ground of our being. The ground will not be the same for all people.
6. Begin with prayer and end with prayer, even if it is just a time to be really quiet.
7. Have an anniversary a year after your last session. See if anything changed.

DONNA SCHAPER

The Rev. Dr. Donna Schaper, formerly at Coral Gables Congregational Church in Miami and before that at Yale University, is Senior Minister for Judson Memorial Church on the corner of Washington Square Park in Greenwich Village, New York City. She began this post in 2005, was ordained 40 years in 2014. As an elder, she is passionately concerned about leaving the next generation well-prepared for all they have to face.

Schaper's purpose in life is to provide spiritual nurture for public capacity. She likes to "kick hope into high gear" and show people what is possible through the magnificence of human community strategically focused and spiritually filled. Her plan at Judson is to be a steward of an extraordinary legacy and to carry the church into the 21st century in terms of organization, vision, resources, and courage. Schaper is no stranger to controversy, having led her Miami congregation through an institutional transformation that opened it to gays, Jews, anti-war protests, significant membership growth and fund and fun raising on behalf of the poor and outcast. Her 31 published books tell the tale of her interfaith marriage, her pioneering journey as an ordained woman, her quiet spirituality and noisy activism. One of the first women trained by Saul Alinsky, the founder of community organization strategies, Schaper has focused on issues of political and economic development and interfaith and open rituals which support action for social change. At Judson she has pioneered work with the New York City New Sanctuary Movement to protect those immigrants being detained or deported unjustly as well as making Judson a home for Occupy and Occupy Faith. She has continued Judson's legacy as a haven for women who insist on the right to choose an abortion and opened the building to countless groups, including Hudson River Clearwater, Domestic Workers and Sex workers organizations, while maintaining its work on harm reduction kits, support for GLBTQ people and especially for homeless gay youth. She has initiated cooperation with NYU, especially through its Spiritual Life Center, now across the street, and has pioneered multifaith liturgy with the campus ministries at NYU. She has presided over a growing congregation and Sunday School and developed a community ministry program which has, over seven years, a total of 43 year-long interns who are prepared to do Judson's brand of public ministry from a parish base. She has also nurtured the arts through Bailout Theater, a site for emerging artists to perform in a cabaret atmosphere, while also bringing free food to the growing numbers who come, and developed the "Gym at Judson," a work-out space for the arts.

Wood Lake

Imagining, living, and telling the faith story.

WOOD LAKE IS THE FAITH STORY COMPANY.

It has told:

- The story of the seasons of the earth, the people of God, and the place and purpose of faith in the world
- The story of the faith journey, from birth to death
- The story of Jesus and the churches that carry his message.

Wood Lake has been telling stories for more than 30 years. During that time, it has given form and substance to the words, songs, pictures, and ideas of hundreds of storytellers.

Those stories have taken a multitude of forms – parables, poems, drawings, prayers, epiphanies, songs, books, paintings, hymns, curricula – all driven by a common mission of serving those on the faith journey.